# A Rage To Live
## *Surviving The Holocaust So Hitler Would Not Win*

This book is dedicated to all the victims and survivors of the ethnic cleansings and genocides that have affected so many lives. It is dedicated to those in England and Scotland, of whom "The Boys" all share the same sentiment when any of us says "They turned us into human beings again." It is also dedicated to the '45 Aid Society for the work they have done and continue to do through The Second Generation.

Copies of our book have been accepted into the Yad Vashem Library in Jerusalem, The Imperial War Museum in London, The St. Petersburg Fla. Holocaust Museum, The Holocaust Outreach Center-Florida Atlantic University-Boca Raton Fla., Terezin Holocaust Memorial Library, Shoah Museum/Library Paris, The US Holocaust Memorial Library in Washington D.C., Eldred WWII Museum and others.

*My copy has arrived, Mr. Krygier. What a superb job you did. As a person who has worked on the contemporaneous as well as memoiristic writings from the Lódz Ghetto for many years, I certainly congratulate you for making this valuable contribution to the literature. Thank you and all best wishes.*
Alan Adelson - Executive Director
Jewish Heritage

*Although I knew about some of Victor's experiences because of his entries on the Lódz KehilaLinks website, this book captures what a truly incredible person he was during the hardest period and at such a young age. His sense of honor, compassion, and generosity through out his life, especially given what he's gone through, are commendable. He and Joe are a perfect fit. I look forward to attending the play, Chagrined, that will be based on the book. Mazel Tov to both of you!! Kudos!*
Roni Seibel Liebowitz – President
Jewish Genealogical Society, Inc. (NY)

*A Rage to Live made me feel like I was sitting in a diner with Victor Breitburg hearing his account of the Holocaust. What I like about him is that he sits comfortably without dwelling on sadness, and his past suffering only prefaces his present and future. From the ghetto to freedom and on to good works and forgiveness, Victor's Rage to Live is an inspiration.*
Pastor J. Shearhart  ★★★★★ Amazon

*I started your book this morning and finished this afternoon, couldn't put it down, Yasher Koach (ask Victor if you don't know what this means.) I have read dozens of books on the Holocaust and have known hundreds of survivors, so there was nothing new for me in Victor's story, but the way you both told his story was very unique. You were able to be succinct yet thorough and very connected emotionally. The chronology was easy to follow and Victor's post Holocaust story made him even more identifiable. I think that this book would be excellent in the beginning of any Holocaust study, particularly in public schools. Because Victor doesn't go into detail on all of the horrors and trauma he experienced before, during and after the War, it is as gentle a way as possible to begin studying the Shoa. Thank you so much for sharing A Rage to Live with me. I plan on having my grandsons read it when they begin studying the Holocaust in Hebrew school.* Ed Finklestein

*Why did I have to read this book to know that the "day that will live in infamy" included the first act of Hitler's "final solution"? I was sitting outside reading, in the shade of a big old tree, and I read the lines several times. I immediately wondered if the Nazis and Japanese had an agreement. I mourn the children that were "resettled." I mourn those who went into the ovens. And I mourn the youth of Victor Breitburg, because he never got to have one. To see his mother and his siblings turn to the right and disappear forever must have been unbearable; but I admire his strong survival instinct and his ability to work hard on almost no food and no encouragement. For a moment I was reminded of Ivan Denisovitch. When the young Hungarian boy was shot for gleaning a spoon of sugar, Victor asks, "Where was the almighty to permit things like this to happen?" Well, where? I wondered if Victor has any real faith in God, after what he went through .I don't have many criticisms of this fine book ... I loved the explanation of Diana Lubarsky's sculptures."* 20th Annual Writer's Digest Annual Self-Published Book Awards:Judge Number: 34

# Acknowledgements

I would like to thank all my friends from Suburban Temple/Temple B'Nai Torah in Wantagh, N.Y. for helping me over the years. So much of what I have done beyond my career was through the Temple. I am grateful to Dr. Regina White, an educator and friend, for providing me with many speaking opportunities. Morton Held, you supported me in all my endeavors and Herman Wiener, you have been my faithful friend. Never forgotten and truly missed is Paul Schiffers. Thank you Seymour Regent, my best bowling partner. Thank you Arthur Ofstowski, my partner in the Bagel Store.

I also thank all my friends in London, England. Ben Helfgot, our chairman of the '45 Aid Society, for publishing *The Return To Lódz* in our journal, which was the most successful of my autobiographical articles. It helped me to begin to think about putting my articles together in a book, at least for my family. Thank you Shirley Ratbajn for encouraging me through many hours of discussion about writing after that article was published. I am grateful to Roni Seibel Liebowitz, with Jewish Records Indexing-Poland and JewishGen, for all your support and for publishing more of my articles.

Thank you Joe. You brought more out of me than I ever wrote. You organized, edited and wrote additional material to make this memoir a reality. We are friends for life.

Victor

I thank my dear wife Deborah. I thank you for your encouragement during the process of completing this project and for spending one week with Victor and me recording video interviews and taking pictures. The pictures that document this project would not exist if you had not been with us. Your help with continuous proofreading and input regarding editing in the final weeks of preparing the manuscript was invaluable before sending it for final formatting.

I am grateful to Roni Seibel Leibowitz, from Jewish Records Indexing-Poland and JewishGen, for referring me to Victor as I was doing research for writing my play (still a work in progress), and for the encouraging words about the book and the play. Thank you for letting me get to know more about your work, and family during our correspondence.

Many thanks to Lee Wilkof, Moe and Karan Bergeron and Rabbi Micah Greenstein, for reading excerpts and making encouraging comments on the play and/or the book in their early stages. Thank you Jack Jeffery, for needed comments and annotations. Thank you Duane Tucker, for allowing me to use a line from your poem, *Boats of Silver*, as a section heading. Paul Gast, thank you for your insight, comments, discussions, dinner and the interview you did with me on teaching the Holocaust. You have helped to make this whole experience an unforgettable one.

Thank you Ruth, for letting me get to know you and for giving up some of your time in attending teas, music nights, some other meetings, all the varied discussions and lots of hugs. I am especially grateful for you providing double chocolate ice cream for two guys at such a late hour. Thank you Denise and Myra Breitburg, for your encouragement and comments during this process.

I would also like to thank my brothers and sisters at New Covenant Baptist Fellowship for their prayers and support.

Thank you Victor, for enriching my life by being my friend. I am grateful that you allowed me to enter into your world, with full access to the story of your life, your home, your friends and your daily routines during the weeks we spent together at Wynmoor. These are cherished memories, not only of working on the book, but because we enjoyed being with each other. L'Chaim.

Joe

# About The Cover and The Sculpture Photos

D. K. Lubarsky was born in Brooklyn, New York in April 1945. She was a physical therapist for 46 years before retiring in early 2010. She and her husband Elliot currently live in a suburb of Portland, Oregon. Diana is neither a survivor of the Holocaust, nor the child of a survivor. She maintains that religious practice was a very minor part of her childhood, and was raised knowing virtually nothing about that time in history.

Her personal involvement with the Holocaust began in 1974, shortly after the birth of her first child. It began with a number of unexplainable nightmares of Nazi Occupation. Over the ensuing years those nightmares evolved into visions, or what Diana calls images. The sculptures in her collection are all representative of the specific lives or images that she has envisioned; hence the title of the exhibit: Holocaust Images.

Diana never pursued any formal art training, but as a hobby had always loved the feel of clay in her hands. The sudden and urgent need to sculpt arrived only after the Holocaust images began. "As image after image seared across my mind, the need to create that which I 'saw' became overwhelming. I was probably more surprised than anyone by the powerful sculptures that flowed from my hands, beginning as early as 1976."

All of the sculptures in the Holocaust Images collection, with the exception of two pieces, have been created from this inner vision. There are two exceptions that were influenced by specific concentration camps that she and her husband visited in 1997.

It is important to note that Diana does not try to reproduce any of the horrific scenes associated with the Holocaust. Instead, she establishes memorials. With the unfaltering guidance of "the people in my head", she remembers a people who could not leave their mark on the world the way they would have chosen; with love, hope, and dignity, all in a setting of Holocaust. "I visualize them, and 'hear' their silent pleas to be remembered. And I remember them, one at a time, with every sculpture I create."

Please visit Diana's website at holocaustimages.org or http://www.holocaustimages.com. By enlarging the individual photographs you will also be able to access the poems that accompany each piece of work as well as the dimensions and construction material. The poems for the pictures in this volume are included in the book in the EXTRAS section.

David Lubarsky (www.DavidLubarsky.com) provided the color cover and interior photographs in high quality, black and white reproductions from the original color negatives of his photographs. David's studio is in New York City where he has been working as an independent assignment photographer for 25 years. Please visit his website.

Cover & interior photographs ©David Lubarsky.

## Other Photos

Mr. Harvey Drucker provided The Holocaust Memorial and Holocaust Torah Cover. He is a member of Temple B'Nai Torah/Suburban Temple in Wantagh, New York. For a beautiful color picture of the Torah Cover visit www.tolifeink.com and http://ny021.urj.net.torah.shtml.

All other photos: © Joseph G.Krygier.

# Introduction

The Holocaust is an inexhaustible topic for research and study. Many who speak about the Holocaust, including Victor, will say it was not just our Holocaust, because of its far-reaching affect on the world. However, the context of the deliberate Jewish Holocaust, of which there are detractors, cannot ever and should not in any way be demeaned.

Genocide didn't originate with the Nazis; it has been a common practice for thousands of years in all parts of the world. The Assyrians and the Babylonians, while attempting to conquer the world, as they knew it, practiced ethnic cleansing by: killing, forced enculturation and deconstructing cultures. Israel was not their only objective. Babylon also had her eyes on Egypt. These ancient cultures were experts at dismantling the societies of those they dominated. The Babylonian scorched earth policy and the deportation of the conquered are examples of how this was accomplished.

In the early twentieth century, there was the greatly debated and contested Armenian Genocide, prosecuted by the Turks. It is widely acknowledged as one of the first modern genocides. Scholars point to the systematic, organized manner in which the killings were carried out to eliminate the Armenians. It is the second most studied case of genocide after the Holocaust. It is still a very sensitive topic. This year, the French Senate passed a law outlawing the denial of the Armenian genocide.

Previous persecutions against the Jews in Western and Eastern Europe, including the pogroms in Russia, were not as widespread as the Holocaust.

The term genocide antedated the contemporary use of the word Holocaust. Raphael Lemkin, a Polish legal scholar, introduced the term genocide. He fashioned the word in 1944 to describe the systematic annihilation of entire groups of people by Nazi Germany during World War II. Scholars estimate that during the last half of the twentieth century, genocide has been committed or attempted by at least sixteen nations in Africa, Central and South America, Asia and Europe.

Holocaust, when specifically applied to the elimination of people, is a modern interpretation of a word found in the Mosaic Law. The anglicized form comes from the Greek word *holoskaustos*. This is the Greek translation of the Old Testament (the Septuagint) Hebrew word, *olah*. The definition is "that which goes up"—the burnt offerings— often translated as "completely burnt" in English. Early rabbinic literature, such as the Mishnah, includes traditions and discussions of the burnt offerings. There have been other references and uses of the word from antiquity to the present. The current use as a noun, with a capitalized H, came into prominence since the war crimes trials after WWII and even more so into the 1950's. Today, the standard use of the word is Holocaust or the Holocaust.

The Hebrew word *sho'ah* (Shoah), used to describe the same event, has an interesting etymology. A "whirlwind of destruction" is the connotation of sho'ah. It was first used in 1940 to refer to the extermination of Jews in Europe in a booklet published in Jerusalem by the United Aid Committee for the Jews in Poland. The booklet was titled *Sho'at Yehudei Polin* (The Holocaust of the Jews of Poland). By 1942 it was more widely used and subsequently, the prefix Ha ("The" in Hebrew) was added. Yom HaShoah, corresponding to 27 Nissan in the Hebrew calendar, is *Holocaust and Heroism Remembrance Day*. It was established in Israel in 1953. It is the day the Jewish Community remembers those who perished. The day also acknowledges the active Jewish Resistance during that period, such as the Warsaw Ghetto uprising. *International Holocaust Day* occurs on January 27 each year. It was inaugurated by a United Nations resolution in 2005 to commemorate the day Auschwitz-Bierkenau was liberated in 1945.

The word Holocaust has been appropriated by many to describe ethnic and other atrocities, and not without controversy. These include African-Americans, Native Americans, Aids Activists and even Environmentalists. Alan Rosenbaum, a professor of philosophy at Cleveland State University and the editor of the anthology: *Is The Holocaust Unique?: Perspectives on Comparative Genocide* (Westview, 1996) has commented on this debate:

*Any attempt by any group to keep a monopoly on language is doomed to failure, because anybody can use any language 2 they want. And the term Holocaust has such power—as the paradigm case of genocide—that any group wanting to make a superlative case for its own experience would naturally want to borrow it.[1]*

There were pre and post WWII atrocities: The Namibian (Herero) Genocide, The Armenian Genocide, Stalin's Genocide of Ukranians and others, The Rape of Nanking by the Japanese, Mao's Cultural Revolution/Great Leap Forward and the Cambodian Killing Fields. The pattern of the Nazi's premeditated Holocaust, their term was the final solution, was similar to the intent and structure of the Armenian genocide. First, intellectuals and community leaders were arrested and executed. The next targeted groups were forced from their homes, marched for hundreds of miles being deprived of food and water and taken somewhere to be summarily executed. Massacres were indiscriminate of age or gender. In Nanking and more recent incidents, rape and other sexual abuse was commonplace.

The number of people murdered by the Nazis is less than Stalin's forced starvations, Gulags and other means, or Mao's deliberate famine. However, the specific intent to implement a final solution for Jews, and to rid the Reich of a national people, the Poles, was something that makes the Holocaust unique. Roma (Gypsies), Jehovah's Witnesses and homosexuals were also specifically targeted throughout Europe. It must be remembered that this genocide, unlike the others, was occurring just before and during a world war. It was not an internal, tribal or regional conflict such as recent atrocities like those in Rwanda, the Baltics, Sudan, Darfur and Myanmar (Burma). This was an intentional, trans-national attempt to eliminate people and their cultures from whatever would be the ultimate boundaries of the Third Reich.

No one will ever have completely accurate figures concerning deaths in the ghettos and camps, but the accepted number is roughly nine million over all and six million of them were Jews. When we

---

[1] Samuel G. Freedman, *Laying Claim To Sorrow Beyond Words, New York Times*, accessed January 15, 2011, http://www.nytimes.com/1997/12/13/movies/laying-claim-to-sorrow-beyond-words.html.

consider that three of those six million were Polish Jews and two of the nine million were Poles: Catholics, Christians and others—that figure is significant. The Holocaust was a defining moment in history for the Jews, and how the world has and still relates to them.

Growing up in the 1950's had a great influence on my emerging worldview and my desire to learn more about history. I always loved reading. We subscribed to Life, Look, The Saturday Evening Post, Reader's Digest and Popular Mechanics (my father's favorite). At the age of ten, I became a member of the Young Reader's Book Club, founded by Bennett Cerf through Random House. It was a birthday present from my mother. I began collecting both Landmark and World Landmark books and I still have my copies of *Alexander Hamilton and Aaron Burr* and *The Marquis De Lafayette*.

My father had a great interest in history and the advent of television in our home became a tool for learning and entertainment. I was born in the modern media age and in 1950, television was beginning to be seen as a major factor in the entertainment and news industries. This whole new world of news, documentaries and movies heightened my learning experience. My first encounters with documentaries about WWII, for example, were the result of sitting with my father watching CBS or NBC special programs. By 1964, Marshal McLuhan opined that we were in the age of the "global village" as a result of communication via electronic media.

In 1960, the last Playhouse 90 production was *In the Presence Of My Enemies*, written by Rod Serling. This captivating drama reveals a realistic and multifaceted view of the Jewish experience in the Warsaw ghetto. Rod Serling was also responsible for these chilling phrases that haunted me as a young boy on *The Twilight Zone*:

"My name is Talky Tina … and I'm going to kill you!"

"I believe you're going … my way?"

"Room for one more honey."

"Jump, Edward … jump!"

However, there were two other *Twilight Zone* episodes that captivated the attention of this 11 year old. *Death's Head Revisited*, broadcast in the 1961-1962 season, tells the story of Captain Gunther Lutze, a former concentration camp leader, who returns to visit his homeland after a seventeen-year absence. Something moves Lutze to go back and revisit his old haunts. He changes his name, takes new residence on the other side of the world and does all he can to forget the harm he inflicted on fellow human beings as a result of "just trying to follow orders." Within a span of two hours he undergoes a transformation from being a power-drunk braggart to a raving maniac. The insanity that he'd kept suppressed for so long could not be contained any longer and he dies after confronting the "ghost" of the Dachau caretaker.

*He's Alive,* broadcast in the 1963 season, tells the story of neo-Nazi Peter Vollmer, who falls victim to a world of hatred and neglect and becomes a cold-blooded, depraved soul, who thrives on political demonstrations. He makes sure the whole world knows of his beliefs. At the advice of his allies, Vollmer kills Ernst, a Jewish Holocaust survivor, who had given him a home years ago when his own parents were viciously fighting. It is up to the viewer to decide whether or not the illusion of Adolf Hitler and Vollmer's conversations with him are only hallucinations. In the end, Vollmer is shot and killed.

In September 1961, *Saturday Night at The Movies* premiered on NBC. On November 9th, 1963 there was the first showing of the 1959 film version of *The Diary of Ann Frank.* This was a larger exposure to the Holocaust. As I got older I saw *Judgment at Nuremburg, The Pawnbroker* and *Exodus.* I also read *The Rise and Fall of the Third Reich* and other books. It seemed to me, that this was a world event that was going to take a lifetime to document, let alone attempt to study.

In 1973, an episode of *The World at War,* narrated by Laurence Olivier was dedicated completely to the Holocaust. The 1978 NBC miniseries, *Holocaust,* possibly more than any other previous film on American television, heightened the consciousness level concerning the Holocaust, although not without controversy. The miniseries won several awards and received critical acclaim, but there was also criticism. This included noted Holocaust author and survivor Elie Wiesel, who described it as "untrue and offensive" in an April, 1978 New York Times article, *Trivializing the Holocaust: Semi-Fact and Semi-Fiction.*

Controversy within the Jewish community, concerning the Holocaust, was and is nothing new. On September 6, 1946 Ben

Hecht's play, *A Flag Is Born*, premiered on Broadway. The cast included a young, unknown actor named Marlon Brando. It was an indictment of American Jews concerning the Holocaust.

Dr. Rafael Medoff cites a number of interesting points about this controversy:

*What is not widely known is that Brando was one of the first public figures in post-World War II America to speak out about the failure of the Allies to aid Europe's Jews during the Holocaust. Brando's platform was the Broadway stage. In the summer of 1946, barely a year after the liberation of the Nazi death camps, 22 year-old Brando co-starred in "A Flag Is Born," an explosive play authored by Ben Hecht, the famed Hollywood screenwriter and Jewish activist. Set in a cemetery in postwar Europe, "Flag" focuses on two elderly Holocaust survivors, Tevya (Paul Muni) and Zelda (Celia Adler), who encounter Brando's character, a distraught young Treblinka survivor named David who is on his way to British-ruled Palestine. Through the conversations between Tevya and David, Hecht articulates the Jewish right to the Holy Land and the need for a Jewish state.*

This article also mentions that:

*During the play, Brando's character speaks of the world's silence while the Nazis 'made a garbage pile of my people.' He also raises pointed questions about the response of Jews in the Free World. One of the most memorable scenes has Brando's character addressing the Jews of the United States and Great Britain. Beginning in a quiet voice and then growing louder, Brando demands: 'Where were you Jews? 'Where were you when the killing was going on? Where was your voice crying out against the slaughter?' We didn't hear any voice. There was no voice. You Jews of America! You Jews of England! Strong Jews, rich Jews, high-up Jews; Jews of power and genius! Where was your cry of rage that could have filled the world and stopped the fires? Nowhere! Because you were ashamed to cry out as Jews.'*

*The accusation sent chills through the audience. Brando later recalled 'At some performances, Jewish girls got out of their seats and screamed and cried from the aisles in sadness, and at one, when I asked, 'Where were you when six million Jews were being burned to death in the ovens of Auschwitz?', a woman was so over come with anger and guilt that she rose and shouted back at me, 'Where were YOU?' ... At the time there was a great deal of soul-searching within the Jewish community over whether they had done enough to stop the slaughter of their people—some argued that they should have applied pressure on President Roosevelt to bomb Auschwitz, for example—so the speech touched a sensitive nerve.*[2]

In a document titled: *The Holocaust Victims Accuse: Documents and Testimony on Jewish War Criminals* by Reb Moishe Schonfeld, some very startling accusations are made. Orthodox rabbis accuse the secular Zionists of helping the cause of the Holocaust by being very selective in who was chosen in the ghettos and other places to survive and to go and build Israel after the war. The exchanges at times are vitriolic:

*Rabbi Chaim Sonnenfeld, chief rabbi of the Orthodox community in the Holy Land, once had a poignant encounter with one of Palestine's leading Zionists. This deliberate opponent of Torah gloried in perpetrating wickedness against the sainted Rabbi Sonnenfeld. Encountering Rabbi Sonnenfeld as the latter left his house with head buried in his hands, after hearing of the untimely death of one of his beloved sons, who was then only 45 years of age, the wicked atheist approached Rabbi Sonnenfeld while he was walking*

---

[2] Dr. Rafael Medoff, "When Marlon Brando Taught The Holocaust", *The David S. Wyman Institute For Holocaust Studies*, April 2004, accessed October12, 2010, http://www.wymaninstitute.org/articles/2004-04-brando.php.

*with deep heartache along the streets of Old Jerusalem. "You are deserving this punishment," mocked the Zionist, "because you have made it your life purpose to fight against us". The Rabbi Sonnenfeld firmly replied, "on the contrary, I am being punished because I have not done enough to destroy your ways. I promise to oppose more vigorously your detrimental way of life.[3]*

This tension and disparity is also found in fiction, as seen in this excerpt from *The Chosen*:

*Danny was not to see me, talk to me, listen to me, be found within four feet of me. My father and I had been excommunicated from the Saunders family. If Reb Saunders even once heard of Danny being anywhere in my presence, he would remove him immediately from the college and send him to an out-of town yeshiva for his rabbinic ordination. There would be no college education, no bachelor's degree, nothing, just a rabbinic ordination. If we tried meeting in secret, Reb Saunders would find out about it. My father's speech had done it. Reb Sanders didn't mind Danny reading forbidden books, but never would he let his son be the friend of the son of a man who was advocating the establishment of a secular Jewish state run by Jewish goyim.[4]*

In a personal way, I had an immersion into Jewish culture during the summer of 1972. I was a member of the Cortland Repertory Theater in central New York. One of the three shows I was in that summer was *Fiddler On The Roof*. I played Avram, the bookseller, and I was a bottle dancer. I got to sing those wonderful songs like Tradition, Sunrise Sunset, and Anatevka for the entire season. A highlight of that production was during early rehearsals for the wedding scene. A Rabbi helped us stage

---

[3] Reb M. Shonfeld, *The Holocaust Victims Accuse* (New York: B'NAI YESHIVOS, 1977), 5-6.

[4] Chaim Potok, *The Chosen* (New York: Ballantine Books 1996), 230.

the wedding scene and explained the significance of the various parts of the ceremony.

When studying the Holocaust, I don't think you can be overtly judgmental of the perpetrators of the crimes while gathering information. You might be so overcome with anger and horror that you will not get very far with your research. Attempting to understand the justification from first hand accounts of politicians, soldiers, camp guards, SS, doctors in the ghettos and the camps, Nazi collaborators in the various countries and so on, is not easily managed. One such account is *KL Auschwitz-Seen By The SS*, a volume that is only available from the Auschwitz/Bierkenau Museum bookstore. If one is not careful, it may lead to a morbid curiosity. I think of Stephen King's story and the subsequent film, *Apt Pupil*, about a young man who becomes obsessed with a former Nazi and how it ends with frightening results.

Today, there is an increasing amount of firsthand testimony from survivors. This is due, in part, to sharing between survivors and their grandchildren. Some of this can be attributed to: the increase of curriculums in public schools, Holocaust Remembrance programs, visiting the Holocaust Museum in Washington, D.C. and other libraries and visitor centers at state, local and regional levels. There are at least three theater companies in the US that exclusively produce plays about the Jewish experience. There are film festivals, book fairs and conferences all year long. There are organizations such as the '45 Aid Society, founded in 1963 in the UK, to help survivors. It grew out of a youth organization called The Primrose Club. They host the yearly reunions of "The Boys" and publish a Journal, which according to Ben Helfgott, "has given us a public profile, a collective voice, and evinced the community at large how we came through our trauma with dignity and independence." (60th Anniversary Edition, Chairman's comments. Ben is also the founder). These voices, speaking about and documenting their experiences is so important, because many of them have so few years left on this earth.

Internet research is almost limitless but not always accurate. Many museums have interactive online pages with audio/video and printed material. Books concerning the Holocaust seem to be published in cycles of interest depending on the approach and the content to be covered. I shared some of these thoughts with Roni

Seibel Leibowitz, from Jewish Records Indexing-Poland and JewishGen, and she responded via email:

> *You bring up several good points about how the Holocaust is viewed today, why people are talking more about it now, why it is unique despite all the other atrocities committed by "civilized" people in history that have taken place, and still do. I like that you argue that we should try to understand the perpetrators, what led people to behave this way to other human beings.*

If this subject is of interest to anyone, I suggest that you be intentional in developing relationships with Holocaust survivors or others who are well versed in the subject. Most of these people will, most likely, be Jewish. Here, in Buffalo, N.Y., there are Gentile Poles who survived, and in 2010 they organized a small conference to publicly share their experiences. These Poles were the specific targets of elimination, as were the Jews. They were not merely "victims" of WWII.

Under these circumstances, it is hard to believe that there were some Poles who still directed their personal animosity and prejudice toward Jews during and after the war. Perhaps the most infamous post war episode was the Kielce incident, when the residents, including policemen, soldiers and boy scouts, murdered 80 Jews. During the war many were just frightened for their own lives because Poles were the only people who were summarily executed for helping Jews. Ironically, Poland is listed as the country with the highest number of Jews saved (6,195) as listed in *The Righteous Among the Nations-per Country & Ethnic Origin: January 1, 2010* at the Yad Vashem Memorial in Israel.

Nazi ideology viewed Slavs as a racially inferior group. September 1, 1939 began the invasion of Poland. Hitler gave explicit permission to his commanders to kill "without pity or mercy, men, women, and children of Polish descent or language." Genocide was conducted, systematically, against all Poles. The voices of hatred and violence continued to peak as noted by Piotrowski:

> *On September 7, 1939 Reinhart Heydrich stated that 'all Polish nobles, clergy and Jews were to be killed' and on September 12,*

*Wilhelm Keitel added intelligentsia to the list. At the end of 1940, Hitler demanded liquidation of 'all leading elements in Poland' and on March 15, 1940 Himmler stated 'All Polish specialists will be exploited in our military-industrial complex. Later, all Poles will disappear from this world. It is imperative that the great German nation considers the elimination of all Polish people as its chief task.[5]*

When these voices are combined with others, you have a cacophony that expresses a full-orbed position concerning Poland's ultimate fate by these tyrants. It is no wonder that Poland and her Jews suffered more losses than any nation as a direct result of genocide.

In a speech delivered by Hitler in Salzburg on 7 or 8 August 1920 at an NSDAP meeting, he said:

*For us, this is not a problem you can turn a blind eye to—one to be solved by small concessions. For us, it is a problem of whether our nation can ever recover its health, whether the Jewish spirit can ever really be eradicated. Don't be misled into thinking you can fight a disease without killing the carrier, without destroying the bacillus. Don't think you can fight racial tuberculosis without taking care to rid the nation of the carrier of that racial tuberculosis. This Jewish contamination will not subside, this poisoning of the nation will not end, until the carrier himself, the Jew, has been banished from our midst.[6]*

Robert Ley's words are documented:

*We swear we are not going to abandon the struggle until the last Jew in Europe has been exterminated and is actually dead. It is not enough to isolate the Jewish enemy of*

---

[5] Thaddeus M. Piortrowski, *Poland's Holocaust* (Jefferson, North Carolina: McFarland & Company, Inc., 1998), 23.

[6] David Irving, *Hitler's War and The War Path* (Duke Street, London, England: Focal Point Publications, 2002), 2.

*mankind-the Jew has got to be exterminated. The second German secret weapon is anti-Semitism, because if it is consistently pursued by Germany, it will become a universal problem which all nations will be forced to consider.*[7]

Adolf Hitler pronounced:

*From the rostrum of the Reichstag, I prophesied to Jewry that, in the event of war's proving inevitable, the Jew would disappear from Europe. That race of criminals has on its conscience the two million dead of the First World War, and now already hundreds and thousands more. Let nobody tell me that all the same we can't park them in the marshy parts of Russia! Who's worrying about our troops? It's not a bad idea by the way, that public rumor attributes to us a plan to exterminate the Jews. Terror is a salutary thing.*[8]

Reinhard Heydrich at the Wannsee Conference, January 20, 1942 in Berlin declared:

*To take the place of emigration, and with the prior approval of the führer, the evacuation of the Jews to the East has become another possible solution. Although both courses of action [emigration and evacuation] must, of course, be considered as nothing more than ... temporary expedients, they do help to provide practical experience which should be of great importance in view of the coming Endlösung (final solution) of the Jewish question.*[9]

---

[7] Robert Ley, "The Trial of the Major War Criminals Before the International Military Tribunal", Vol.3, Nuremberg, 1947, p. 36, accessed November 16, 2009, http://www.loc.gov/rr/frd/Military_Law/NT_major-war-criminals.html.

[8] Adolf Hitler, "Hitler's Table Talk", (October 1941), quoted in John Toland, *Adolf Hitler* (London: Book Club Associates, 1977), 702-703.

[9] A. J. Mayer, *Why Did the Heavens Not Darken: The "Final Solution" in History* (London: Verso, 1990) 304.

In Berlin, on September 30, 1942 Adolf Hitler reminded his audience:

*There was a time when the Jews in Germany also laughed at my prophecies. I do not know whether they are still laughing today, or whether they have been cured of laughter. But take my word for it: they will stop laughing everywhere.*[10]

The Russians invaded northeastern Poland in 1939, and perpetrated the mass executions at Katyn in 1940, which they denied for years by implicating the Nazi's. In 1990, the Kremlin officially accepted responsibility for the murders. Although hidden for all those years, the event was documented in the public records.

The number of victims is estimated at about 22,000. The victims were murdered in the Katyn Forest in Russia, the Kalinin and Kharkov prisons and elsewhere. About 8,000 were officers taken prisoner during the 1939 Soviet invasion of Poland. Polish doctors, professors, lawmakers, police officers and other public servants were arrested for allegedly being intelligence agents, gendarmes, landowners, saboteurs, factory owners, lawyers, officials and priests. Since Poland's conscription system required every non-exempt university graduate to become a reserve officer, the NKVD (the Soviet secret police) was able to round up much of the Polish intelligentsia, and the Russian, Ukrainian, Tatar, Jewish, Georgian, and Belarusian intelligentsia of Polish citizenship. More detail can be found in: *Death in the Forest: The Story of the Katyn Forest Massacre,* by Janusz K. Zawodny.

Ethnic cleansing and genocide are not going away. Asking why and attempting to find an answer will be based on the pre-suppositions of your worldview. Even then there may still be difficulties, depending on whether or not you accept moral absolutes in your purview.

Eliazar Urbach in his autobiography, *Out of The Fury*, observed:

*During my seven-year odyssey to freedom, I saw a variety of reactions to the Holocaust. Some Jews, like those who attended the Rosh Hashanah service I visited at a Jewish*

---

[10] Mayer, "Final Solution," 344.

*home, clung to faith, but were bewildered at God's silence during Hitler's evil reign of death, Others, particularly young Jews, became atheists, losing faith altogether, and gave themselves over to anger and hatred. Still others fell into a limbo of neither here nor there, unable to deny God's existence completely, but left with a faith so devitalized to restore their broken spirits. Where was God when six million died? The question will continue to be asked. For many Jewish people the belief in an omnipotent, beneficent God became impossible after Auschwitz.[11]*

This is evident in many sources, including an interview with Lipa Tepper, one of "The Boys" who was liberated with Victor and was taken to Windermere, England:

*I started doing something then, which I had never done before, that was to question my beliefs and my reasons for believing. I found that there were insufficient answers to justify a continuation of my former life. I found that everything was destroyed and there was nothing in its place. I looked scornfully at synagogues. I looked scornfully at rabbis, then, I looked scornfully at religion in general. I walked away from it because I refused to believe. More than that, I was terribly, terribly annoyed with God, with religion and everything that it stood for. Life carried on and we left Windermere, which was a very, very good place. We had time to relax and I had time to think, although I realize that emotionally I had not grown up. I found out that a lot of the boys were more advanced in their thinking than I was. I had simply not grown up.[12]*

Urbach goes on to say:

[11] Edith S. Weigand, *Out Of The Fury* (Charlotte, North Carolina: Chosen People Ministries Inc., 1987), 101.

[12] Martin Gilbert, *The Boys* (New York: Henry Holt, 1997), 307-08.

*I began to ask myself, "Can we really blame God for human evil-doing? Is not the real question vis a vis the Holocaust: "Where was humanity when God has "shown you O man what is good; and what does the Lord require of you but to do justice, and to love kindness, and to walk humbly with your God" (Micah 6:8).*[13]

This is part of the great debate addressing the very nature of man and the age-old conversation concerning "the problem of good and evil" and "ethics and morality" in the world. For some, God, even though defined in many ways, comes into the discussion, and for others a deity is irrelevant to the discussion.

It is encouraging to realize that the U.S. now has a formal position on genocide. It can be found in the *Presidential Study Directive on Mass Atrocities:*

*Sixty-six years since the Holocaust and 17 years after Rwanda, the United States still lacks a comprehensive policy framework and a corresponding interagency mechanism for preventing and responding to mass atrocities and genocide. This has left us ill prepared to engage early, proactively, and decisively to prevent threats from evolving into large-scale civilian atrocities ... steps toward creating a comprehensive policy framework for preventing mass atrocities, including but not limited to: conducting an inventory of existing tools and authorities across the Government that can be drawn upon to prevent atrocities; identifying new tools or capabilities that may be required; identifying how we can better support and train our foreign and armed services, development professionals, and build the capacity of key regional allies and partners, in order to be better prepared to prevent and respond to mass atrocities or genocide.*[14]

---

[13] Weigand, "Fury," 102.

[14] Presidential Memoranda, "Presidential Study Directive on Mass Atrocities", accessed 9/24/2011, http://www.whitehouse.gov/the-press-office/2011/08/04/presidential-study-directive-mass-atrocities.

Our hope is, that if a survivor of any genocide reads this book, and can identify in any way with the events that are recorded here, that they will be encouraged to share their story, because every story is worth telling. For those who have not suffered in this way, whether you call it luck, fate, serendipity, karma or God's providence, I encourage you to be more than just an observer of world events and to be engaged with the suffering of your fellow human beings in any way possible; befriend those in need of friends.

There are many ethnic peoples, and within those ethnic peoples there are many cultures that make up this world in which we live. However, we are all of one blood, and of one race—the Human Race.

The Holocaust was an event that was full of horrors and heroism, contradictions and confirmations, apathy and sympathy. Some may question the authenticity of the events of some Holocaust survivors lives, and for that reason, I am particularly attracted to what Elie Wiesel says, "Some stories are true that never happened."

Joseph G. Krygier

# Table of Contents

# Preface

My wife, Lucille, my daughter Myra and I were visiting my daughter Denise, at her college in Phoenix. We decided to take a trip to Los Angeles. To get to Los Angeles we had to drive over a mountain. Along the way, I noticed a horse stable and we stopped. I inquired if there was a trail that could reach the mountain peak. The stable man saddled three horses. Lucille remained behind. A guide from the stable took us to the peak of the mountain and from there we looked at the rim of the Pacific Ocean. We were transfixed by this panorama and I turned to my daughters and said, "Life is beautiful."

# SECTION ONE

## *What Is Past Is Prologue*[15]

The turmoil I've prevailed over reaches throughout eternity.

And yet, I come to enlighten your innocent minds with the wisdom of my experiences.

I make my afflictions known.

I have learned it makes my people stronger.

And I willingly speak of my torture.

I am not a victim.

No, I am a survivor.

Untitled poem written by Sylvia Memendez, after Victor spoke to Mrs. Cohen Willard's 10H English class, at Amityville High School, in April, 2000.

---

[15] Shakespeare, *The Tempest*, II. i.245–254

# Chapter 1

## Long Ago and Far Away

Shlomo Vigdor Wajnman was probably born in Kaminsk, Poland in 1857. He came from a very grand Orthodox Jewish family. I don't know anything about his childhood other than he went to a yeshiva for higher learning. He was capable of writing and reading several languages: Polish, Russian, German, Yiddish, and Hebrew. In town, he was known as "the man who writes letters in several languages," and many Jews and Poles used his skills. He was an exemplary Jew: a Melamed (teacher), husband and conscientious father. He also served in the Russian army during the Russo-Japanese War. He was a man of stature, not only in height, but also in character.

Kaminsk was a shtetl, between Piotrkow and Belchatow, about ninety kilometers south of Lódz. It was a typical shtetl like hundreds of others in Poland. Half the population was Jewish and half was Catholic. Neither group particularly cared for the other. Our harsh life was not discriminatory, and the result was that we tolerated and depended on each other; poverty was our mutual enemy.

In the center of the shtetl was a market. Every Wednesday the Polish farmers brought their commodities there. Money was seldom exchanged; most of the time they bartered as they had done for centuries. On the right side of the market there was a Catholic church, and just a little distance away there was a synagogue.

My grandfather was twenty-three when the family of the Wajnmans and the Magnus' met for the purpose of a betrothal between Shlomo (Victor) Vigdor and Sura (Sarah) Kaila (Kay). A formal engagement was announced, and within one year they were married. At the time of their marriage, Sarah-Kay was fourteen. She was fifteen when their first baby girl was born; they named her Nacha Yita. Eight children joined the family over the next eight years. Even though Shlomo was making a good living, this large family needed some financial help.

3

Grandmother was a petite woman, 4' 11" tall, and weighed about one-hundred pounds. She decided to help out by opening stores in the local markets and selling wares. The shtetls were not too far from one another and each one had its own market on a different day of the week. While she was working, the older children cared for the younger —that was daily life in the shtetl. You could insert our story into *Fiddler on the Roof.* I wonder how many men may have thought like Tevye when he said, "Lord, who made the lion and the lamb—You decreed I should be what I am. Would it spoil some vast eternal plan, if I were a wealthy man?"

There was plenty of affection in the family. The rule of the home was Torah. It was everyone's responsibility to help and serve others, not only members of the family, but anyone in need. In the *Ethics of the Fathers* 1:2, it is written that the world depends on three things: Torah, worship and loving deeds.

On April 12, 1902, my thirty-eight year old grandmother, Sarah, was in labor with her eighth child. With the help of two midwives and some neighboring women, she gave birth to a baby girl, my mother. A week after her birth, the local Rabbi, may he be blessed, after a short service, named my mother Chava (Eve), like Adam's wife. After two weeks, my grandmother went back to the market and her store. She sold dry goods, three days a week. If you are wondering who was taking care of the other seven small children, it was arranged that every older child was responsible for the next youngest, except for the smallest child Chava. She became the responsibility of my grandfather.

Chava often sat on my grandfather's knee watching the students learn to pray, from early morning prayers to evening prayers, and everything between. One day, my grandfather noticed that Chava was moving to the rhythm of the students, and was repeating the prayers just like them. At the age of five, she learned to read and write the Hebraic alphabet. There was no holding back that child. If you saw the movie *Yentl* and remember her ambition to learn the Torah; well, it was the same with my mother.

When my mother was older, my grandfather went to the Rabbi for advice, "Rabbi, what should I do? Chava is now ten years old, and she is teaching herself to read the holy language, also she chants the holy Torah?"

For a while there was silence. "Well, you are not permitted to teach her any more, but you cannot stop her either. She cannot chant or pray in the temple. But if God, may He be blessed, is leading Chava in His own way, none of us should have to stop her." With this edict my grandfather was powerless to stop her from tutoring his students in the regular prayers, but not the Torah"

Six years passed, and Chava had many suitors. Her eyes were looking at a sixteen year old, lanky, blonde haired boy, with the most beautiful blue eyes—which did not escape my grandfather's attention either. Chava, my grandfather said, "I noticed that you are looking at David with a glance in your eyes. Look at him. His shoes are torn, he wears clothes which most probably somebody else wore before him; he is just too young for you."

Well, little Chava always had an answer, "He is sixteen … the same age as I am!" Two weeks later David was in the Polish cavalry; he must have lied about his age. She did not see him for the next three years. Shlomo Vigdor passed away that year, 1918, to the great sorrow of his family and everyone in town. Two of his children, Nacha Yita and Hilda, were not there because they had emigrated to the United States. In 1921, David returned from fighting in WWI and then against the Russians for freedom. Poland, after four hundred years, was again an independent nation. A short time later, David and Chava were married.

# The Next Generation

When my mother was in the late stage of her first pregnancy, my grandmother received a visa from her daughters in America. She'd kept postponing her journey for years because she didn't want to leave until my mother's first child was born. That day arrived on May 8, 1927. Seven days after my birth I was circumcised, according to Mosaic Law, and named Shlomo (Victor) Avigdor after my grandfather. I was the second Shlomo Avigdor named after my grandfather; the first was a cousin. In a small shtetl like Kaminsk, it was always a great event. There were many former students of my grandfather who came to the circumcision, just to touch his grandson.

My grandmother saved some cake from my bris (circumcision celebration) to share with her two daughters in America. When the time came for her to leave, the final goodbyes were said, and my four uncles and my mother assembled at the railroad station to bid her farewell. Tears flowed down their faces. Leaving for the United States was not like it is today. We can travel wherever we want to as long as we have the money to pay for it. In 1927, the borders of the United States were closing for Eastern European Jews. When someone left for America, it was like they were gone for eternity.

She arrived on the shores of America, settled in Brooklyn, New York and remarried. Her second husband was an Orthodox Jewish gentleman and her new name was Sura Kaila Latowitz. She lived a blissful life in her new homeland. Sarah worked with Nacha Yita, earning some extra money, at a place where chickens are prepared before they are inspected and approved as being kosher.

There was not one Passover that my grandmother didn't send some money and gifts to her children in Poland. For two dollars you were able to make a Shabbat for six people. None of us knew that she took the job to save the money to send it to us, along with the gifts.

When I was about five years old, observing my mother in full swing with preparations for Passover, my father went to the post office to pick up a package from America. When he arrived with the package we were eager to see what was inside. It was like a ritual. Once the package was opened, there was something for everyone. There were toys, a jacket for my father and the latest design dresses for my mother. There were many other things including two letters; one was addressed to me. The letters were written in Yiddish, therefore my mother had to read them. My grandmother must not have realized that tears had come down her cheeks as she wrote, and it blotted out the ink on the letters. I didn't understand then, but today I can feel my mother's anguish and pain. Many times I would hug her on Erev Passover to console her saying that someday we all will go to America. Ironically, on April 2, 1939, on Erev Passover, we received a telegram that Sura Kaila, had passed away.

The Holocaust would take its toll on our family. From the children, grandchildren and in-laws of my mother's family, the Wajnmans, only two out of 54 people survived: Reizel (Shoshana, the daughter of Eizel) and myself. Immediately after the war, Reizel was in a DP camp in Germany and eventually was brought to America via the Jewish Resettlement. She eventually married Eric Gotheiner and had two daughters, Helen and Shirley. In 2001 she was physically deteriorating and had no memory. She passed away in 2010.

My father's brother, my Uncle Moses Breitburg, also survived. He and I were the only survivors from Kaminsk. Moses was born in Kaminsk in 1910. He was from a family of tailors. Moses had a wife and 2 young sons before World War II. They were placed in the Lódz Ghetto and then transported to Auschwitz, where his family perished. From there, he was placed in the concentration camp at Dauchau were he was forced to make SS uniforms to survive.

After being liberated from the concentration camp, Moses met Rosa in a displaced persons camp. They were married and lived in Munich, Germany for two years after the war. Two children, Betty and Emanuel were born in Munich. Then they came to the United States by ship entering at Ellis Island. After arriving in the United States they resided in Cincinnati, where he worked as a tailor for the Fetchheimer Factory making uniforms for about twenty five years. He was a great provider to his wife and six children: Betty, Emanuel, Ellen, Sherry, David and Pearl. Moses passed away at the age of sixty in 1971, due to a cerebral hemorrhage while on his break at his job.

In 1994, after some searching, I finally found the grave of my grandmother Sura Kaila. Because of the change of her name with her second marriage, and since the older generation had died many years ago, no one knew her burial place. I brought Reizel's children and my wife to the gravesite. She is buried in Beth David Cemetery in Elmont, Queens N.Y.

One can cry without showing a tear and one can speak without a word being spoken. That is how I felt when I was at her grave. I apologized, over and over again, and said how sorry I was that I was not able to save anyone from her family. I realized it was beyond my capacity to do anything, but the guilt remains. Looking at her grave, I felt that she was listening to me, and at that point I said Kaddish.

# Chapter 2

## Storks, Chickens, Books and Movies

My father left Kaminsk a couple of months after I was born to find a better future for us in Lódz. Many famous people came from Lódz, including Arturo Rubenstein, the great pianist. With a population of over a half-million people, and vibrant textile industries, living in Lódz made finding a job easier than in many places in Poland. Once he returned, there was nothing to entice him to stay in the shtetl; he had no prospects for employment. The decision was made to move to Lódz, where there was more work and better opportunities. When I was six months old, my family packed up all our belongings and we became Lódziers.

My father secured a one-room apartment for us. It had three windows facing the street. We divided the space into three separate rooms. The walls were two feet under the ceiling, so it was still considered one room, otherwise we would have had to pay rent for more. Within four months of resettling, my father opened a tailor shop for ladies coats. It didn't take long before he had five employees. A benefit to this success was moving to a very prestigious street, 11go Listopada 58, on the first floor. Directly in front of the stairs was a nice shiny bell. When I was old enough to go out to play on my own and go to school, I would ring that bell to let everyone on the floor know that I was home.

One room was my father's shop. There was a cutting table and two sewing machines. Depending on the season, there were always two of the five employees working with my father, and at times my mother had to help out. Season notwithstanding I was often underfoot, as I was always fascinated by the trade journals showing the latest styles, which came to us directly from Paris.

We had a small kitchen and a bedroom. I seldom slept in my bed. We always had guests from the shtetl and I wound up sleeping on the floor. When I was old enough to understand, I was told that sleeping on the floor was good because, "This is the way the people in Palestine sleep." I never complained again. Above the beds we had a large painting of Samson, with his muscular arms outstretched, shifting the pillars of the Philistine temple, which supported the whole structure. I always dreamt that someday I would be like Samson.

The complex had a front building with two large doors in the rear. There were two apartment buildings on each side, and the toilet building was all the way in the back. This enclosed the area we called the yard. This was another privilege not to be taken lightly. We were rich by some standards because we had electricity and cold water in our apartment. Can you imagine that … two forty-watt bulbs were luxuries! Our yard was our football stadium, our skating rink and our dreamland. There were over 119 families, all Jewish except the janitor, and each family had more than two children.

In 1931, at the age of four, I was sent to the Cheider (elementary school to learn the basics of Judaism in the melamed's home), which I hated with a passion. It wasn't my studies that I disliked. The melamed was an old man, with a white beard, who always coughed and sneezed. He smoked like a chimney and smelled like a camel. As he tutored us, he constantly exhaled cigarette smoke in our faces and we involuntary inhaled. Those were the days before anyone used a term like "second-hand smoke." We became addicted to smoking. My father also smoked. Between those two people I became a cigarette junkie at the ripe age of four. Well, my father caught me trying to smoke half of his cigarette and I got a shellacking with a belt on my bottom. The good part was, I never had to go back to the Cheider. I got a private tutor at home.

# The Bocian (Stork)

When I was five years old, my mother asked me to come over to her because she had something very important to tell me. "When a woman gets a big stomach, that is a signal that the Bocian is about to bring a baby to her, and most probably it will be here soon. When the time comes, I will tell you to go up on the fourth floor and open the door from the roof and show the Bocian where we live."

As fast I was able to disengage myself from my mother, I ran out into the yard where my friends were and I made an announcement: "My mother is going to get a brand new baby from the Bocian." I told everyone who wanted to listen to me what an important assignment I had.

Every morning, as soon as I got up, the first words from my mouth were, "Mother, is it today?"

"They are not flying today."

"But your stomach is getting bigger."

Every day I asked the same question and every day the answer was the same.

One afternoon, while playing football, I was called by my mother.

"Can't it wait a little longer until we finish playing?"

"No, you have to come right now. The Bocian is starting to fly."

If a boy could run as fast as a lighting bolt comes to the ground, I tried to as I ran up those stairs, opened the door to the roof and was ready to welcome the new brother who would be delivered by the Bocian. I had asked the Rabbi to teach me a prayer to welcome my new brother. I really didn't want to have a sister because when a boy is born, a week later, every one makes a party. There were no parties for girls. I must have been sitting there for hours, and my stomach told me that it was time to have a piece of cake. I ran down into our apartment and announced that I wanted something to eat. There were two women there and they looked like they were doing something to my mother.

I heard my mother, with a cracking voice say, "Take a piece of cake and go up to the roof ... fast." I grabbed the piece of crumb-cake and once again I was sitting in front of the roof door waiting for the Bocian.

One of the women's voices called me, "Victor come down ... your mother wants to talk to you"

"I can't come down because I have to watch the roof door for the Bocian."

"It's alright, come down."

I darted down the stairs, I pushed the door open and cried out, "Why are you calling me, don't you know I might miss the Bocian?"

I looked around the room. Towels were lying around and some of them even had blood on them. The women, with folded arms, were smiling at me. A sheet was strung up around our bed.

"Where is my mommy?" I cried out.

I heard my mother saying that the sheet should be removed. There was my mother and on her head was a wet towel. She was breast-feeding a strange child.

"Where did this child come from," I asked with a whining voice.

"The Bocian brought you a brother."

"Impossible. I never took my eyes of the roof door. You have a strange child. He is not my brother." Tears were running down my face and I kept repeating, "Bocian could not have passed me … a gypsy must have dropped this baby here." For days I told every one that the baby was not my brother. I said a gypsy must have brought him and I didn't want anything to do with him.

After the Bocian incident, my sexual education came from my friends in the yard. I learned that you have to get married; the father has to do it. When I asked what he had to do, every one answered, "You know … he has to do it. When a woman becomes pregnant, the father has to do it many times. The bigger a woman gets, the more times a man has to do it *every* night." This was really advanced biology.

With Felek added to our family, we eventually moved to a larger apartment in the same building, which had three windows in the front. My father had the room divided and my brother and I slept in a bed next to my parents. Of course, we slept on the floor when visitors came.

## *Teaching A Chicken To Fly*

At the age of six my closest friends were Moishe Markowitcz and Motek Lefkowitcz. We also permitted (political correctness was not known in those days) two girls to play with us—Sala Finkelstein and her sister Pola, the shoemaker's daughters.

"What are we going to do," everyone moaned.

"I know!" "We are going up to the attic to feed the chicken. Then we are going to take the chicken to the Shohet (the ritual slaughterer)."

"What chicken?" they all asked.

"The chicken my mother bought for Shabbat tomorrow."

"What does the Shohet do with the chicken?" Moishe asked.

Now I felt like a grown up because I had all the answers. "My mother and I have gone to the Shohet many times, and when he was ready, he told me to turn around and face the western wall. He made a prayer over the chicken, and as soon as he finished, the chicken sacrificed herself for us and lay down to sleep."

All of us went up to the attic on the fourth floor, and there was our walking dinner for Friday night. We fed the chicken, everyone had a turn to hold and play with it, but after a while we got tired and looked for something else to do.

"What are we going to do now?" asked Sala.

In my great wisdom I proclaimed, "How about we teach the chicken to fly?"

Moisho said, "A chicken is too stupid to fly."

"Of course, because nobody takes the time to teach the chicken how to fly. If God didn't want the chicken to fly, then God would not have given the chicken wings. Besides, a chicken *is* a bird."

We took the chicken, sat down on a box, and with a slight push the chicken started to flap its wings and landed on the floor. What a great achievement this was. We actually proved that a chicken could fly.

Next, we put the chicken to a higher level until she was near the ceiling. With a slight push, there went the chicken happily flapping its wings and gently landing down on the floor. I could not hold back any more, "You see … didn't I tell you that all we had to do was teach the chicken to fly."

Then came the final test. I picked up the chicken, and standing on my toes, I put my hand out of the small window and let the chicken go. I think we must have been flying down the stairs as we rushed out to the yard to see if the chicken flew away. What we saw was Mrs. Krupska trying to catch the limping chicken. She screamed at us, and then I noticed my mother standing there. Mrs. Krupska and my mother were successful in catching the chicken, and both of them went into her house. When my mother came out, she gave me a look and it felt like an electric shock went through my body.

"What were you doing with that poor chicken?" she demanded.

Very proudly I said, "We were teaching the chicken how to fly."

That did it! My mother grabbed me by the ear and up I went towards our apartment. She had such a hold on my ear that if she could have thrown me forward and into the air she might have said, "Now it is your turn to try and fly."

The next day was Friday. Mother lit the candles and we all sat down for our normal Friday evening meal. My father started with the prayer over the wine, and then we all said the prayer over the bread, even though it was chala. My mother passed the plate with the sweet carp on it. For the next course, we normally had chicken soup with noodles and topped it with some lima beans. I looked at our plates. There were noodles, and some lima beans, but no chicken soup or chicken.

"Mommy, how come we don't have chicken soup?" I complained.

"Mrs. Krupska has our chicken, because the chicken was not kosher any more."

"Why was the chicken not kosher?"

"Because you taught the chicken how to fly."

"Well, what is wrong with trying to teach chickens how to fly? Don't we teach other animals to do certain things for us?"

"Now listen my huchem … if we teach the chicken how to fly, then she will teach other chickens how to fly, and they will fly away."

"So, what is wrong with that?"

"Nothing, except every Friday I will have to go hunting for the chickens, and I will be darned if I am going to climb trees to get you eggs for your breakfast."

If I had succeeded, what a catastrophe I would have created.

# The Journey Window

I started to attend public school when I was seven years old. It was only two blocks away from where we lived and I could go home for lunch. Even though this was a regular public school, there weren't any Catholic students. I don't know why … perhaps they went to a Catholic school. What I liked most about the school was that I started to learn how to read. A new world opened up for me, and as time progressed, my love for reading took hold of my imagination. On the corner of Zeromskiego there was a news kiosk. Every Wednesday they posted the latest serial stories. I used to pay two groshy for the vendor to let me read behind the kiosk, with the promise that I would keep the magazine clean. Here were my dreams: King Arthur and his Knights, Prince Valiant, Sherlock Holmes and Tarzan.

One evening I was completing my studies and my mother asked, "Shloimelo what are you reading?"

"I am writing about the Polish King, Kasimir IV."

"I know about him-he brought the Jews into Poland."

"That is not quite right; he invited the Jews to settle in Poland and he also put the Jews under his protection."

"When you finish your homework, I would like to talk to you."

Uh-oh, I should not have corrected my mother. There was silence between us and I went back to do my homework. When I finished, I rushed to put on my shoes because I still wanted to play football before it got dark. I completely forgot that my mother wanted to talk to me, but *she* didn't.

"Where are you going? Please sit down," she said sternly.

"I am sorry that I corrected you."

She started to laugh, "If somebody is mistaken, there is nothing wrong in correcting the person, but it must be done very tactfully."

After a moment, to let her words sink in, she said, "I have noticed that you are reading a lot of books … tell me, what do you get out of reading?" I didn't know what my mother meant.

"I read books because I like to read."

"Well, I thought so. You see Shloimelo, a book is like a window. When you read you have to step out from the window and follow the story wherever the author is taking you. He wants you to become a part of his adventure, and if you will permit him, he will open the world before your eyes. Now go play your football."

## My Father's Gift

In 1937, at the age of ten, a new world opened up for me when I was allowed to go to the movies by myself. Every Saturday my father would give me 25 groshy to see the latest cowboy movie, and 10 groshy to take a trolley. Well, for 10 groshy I was able to buy two bars of chocolate and still have some change left. "What is more important, chocolate or the trolley?" No debate was necessary.

I walked to every corner of Lódz where there was an adventure movie playing. Like all kids, we played out what we saw in the movies. After one of the swashbucklers, we made simple swords so we could play at being pirates. It was easy to make. We just needed to fasten together two thin pieces of wood. One day, as we were sword fighting, I stopped and said, "Wait a minute. This is not right."

"What do you mean?" said Motek.

I was thinking that somehow it was not right that two Jewish kids were pretending to fight each other with what looked like crosses. We found some chicken wire and fashioned a hand covering and turned our "cross" swords into pirate sabers.

# Chapter 3

## A Child's Last Vacation

The summer of 1938 is the most cherished memory of my childhood; I was 11 years old. Living in Lódz during the summer was like living in a baker's oven. In a textile town it was common for the factories to operate double-shifts. The smoke from the tall chimneys, mixed with the summer heat, sometimes formed inversions and it became unbearable to live there. I didn't care about the pollution. All I knew was that vacation was approaching and I had passed all my tests with a C+. I had survived the fourth grade with Mr. Kmiecz, my anti-Semitic teacher. This teacher loved to terrorize us. Most of the students were Jewish, but he could not be fired because, like my father, he was a veteran of the First World War and an officer in the reserve of the Polish army. I got off easier with him than others, but even though my father outranked him, it made no difference concerning the classroom.

Our apartment on 11go Listopada 58, between Zeromskiego and Zakatna, was next to an army barracks with a complement of about a thousand soldiers. Normally at this time of the year, they went away for their summer maneuvers. This year they did the training on the premises. It was strange to stand on the roof and watch them as they played war games, using bayonets on dummies while the drums of real war were echoing all around us. On March 12, 1938, Austria was annexed, and became part of greater Germany.

Vacation was the time for most of us to play football until we were exhausted, which at that age, made for long days. My friends and I eagerly anticipated our school vacation, but this summer I had to leave them all behind to spend the summer in the little village of my birth. My parents decided that we were going to spend our summer vacation in Kaminsk. My mother was particularly excited about the prospect of spending the summer there. As soon as the first day of vacation began, we were on our way. My father stayed behind in Lódz and promised he would join us shortly.

# A Child's Last Vacation

We traveled luxuriously by bus. The roads from Lódz to Kaminsk were not well paved, and after six hours of sitting and stopping in several places we arrived. Tired, sleepy and perspiring, we stepped off the bus. My younger brother Felek was six-years-old and was grouchy all through the trip because he had straddled a broken seat. I changed with him several times, but a grouchy kid is a grouchy kid when he wants to be.

My father's sister Yochvah and my uncle Yitzhak were waiting for us at the square in the center of town. After greetings and kissing us several times, we were on our way to their home for the next ten weeks. My Uncle Yitzhak guided us through a street with no lights, to a one-room apartment and lit the naphtha lamp. He said a welcome prayer and a blessing for our safe arrival. He then helped us unpack, and when my brother and I were ready to go to bed, he once again blessed us.

When he left, my mother said, "He is the mirror image of my father." She told me that I was born with a golden spoon in my mouth, and the aura of my grandfather was with me. When I was in her arms I always felt secure.

Coming back to Kaminsk from Lódz was like returning to medieval times; there was no electricity, movies, trolley cars, or theaters. When the naphtha lamp was extinguished, the room was pitch black. Everyone fell asleep except me. All through the night I heard the sound of crickets, which kept me awake. I quietly went over to the door and walked out to see the stars. During the last semester of school we had an introductory course in astronomy. Before this I never had a chance to observe stars in total darkness. I never knew there were so many stars in the sky. I was awe-struck, looking at the stars all around me as though they were trying to touch the ground. I kept turning around and around until I was dizzy. Something majestic must have created such a magnificent panorama. After a while I went into the house and went to sleep.

A couple of days later, I decided to explore Kaminsk. Not far from our place there was a tannery, and the smell was quite strong. I didn't have to know from which direction it came; my nose told me. Even today I can associate that smell with a tannery wherever I am.

# A Rage To Live

On Wednesday, I had to get up early because it was market day. By early dawn you could hear the horse-drawn wagons, with their metal-rimmed wheels, pounding the cobble-stoned street as they brought produce to the market. I was eleven-years old and strong for my age. I decided to solicit the vendors for part-time work. In Lódz, I started to do errands for people to make some extra money during the summer, so I thought, "Why not do the same thing here?" I earned twenty-five groshy (about twenty cents) from each vendor in Lódz. It was the horses that kept me in business back home. I used to feed, clean and brush them. I was never afraid of horses. There was something in me that desired to become acquainted with any horse I encountered. In Kaminsk, whenever there was a group of us looking to do chores or errands, and someone asked, "Who can work with horses?" I immediately raised my hand. It didn't take long before my experience was recognized. In a short time I was getting more work than I could handle, and I enlisted two of my cousins as partners.

My mother's aunt lived past the market, and it was always good to stop at her home, because there was a guarantee to enjoy some milk and crumb cake with every visit. In her house she had a loom. She wove custom textiles. I watched as her fingers moved the special piece of wood that divided the threads. Like magic, the material kept growing. Looking at that woman, I observed that as she worked, she never took her eyes off me. "You look like Yitzhak's son, and all the Shlomo Vigdor's have a certain trait. All of you are very curious." She was right. I wanted to know how things were done and how things were assembled and made to work.

At the market, the Polish farmers sold their crops. The Jews were cabinet-makers, tinsmiths, glaziers, tailors, shoemakers and each hawked their own wares. It was noisy from the goats, cows, chickens and all the other activity. There was even a shochet there. People bargained, and after arriving at an honest price, they smiled because everyone thought that he or she had outwitted the other.

My Uncle Yitzhak owned the mikvah (the ritual immersion bath) and was the gabbai (assistant) of the shul (synagogue/school.) Every Friday morning, all married women went to the mikvah to get ready for Shabbat. The men went in the afternoon. I helped out at the mikvah.

One of the chores for my cousins and me was to hoist water from the well. At the end of a pole, a rope was attached from which a water bucket hung down to fetch the water. On the other end of the pole was a counterweight to help lift the water from the well. I don't remember how many buckets of water we had to bring up to fill the boiler, but it took many hours. How primitive it was to work that way. I used to think, "Why don't they use a simple electric pump?" In spite of my curious nature, what I failed to realize was that naphtha lamps were being used because there was no electricity.

After we finished our chores, I asked my mother, "If I save enough money from my enterprises, can I buy a dog?"

"Wait until your father comes home and we will discuss it."

Within a week, my aunt Sheindel, with her two children, came to Kaminsk. Reizel was one year younger than I was, and her brother Shloimo Vigdor was only four-years-old. Reizel also came from Lódz, but we were very different. She was more of a protected child than I was. While I was able to go the movies by myself, Reizel could not. So, now that she was with us in Kaminsk, I was worried that I was going to lose my new freedom and that I was destined to become her baby sitter. I spoke to my mother about it and after my short speech, my mother in her wisdom said, "I guess you will have to protect her." I knew it.

"Ma," I said with a pleading and whining voice, "Do I have too?" The conversation ended. I said to myself, "It wasn't enough to take care of my brother, now I have to take care of a girl who will follow me wherever I go."

My father and my Uncle Eizel, my mother's brother, came to stay with us for a week. We went over to my Grandfather Emanuel's house. It was a modest three-room brick house. This was the house where my father, my Uncle Moisho and my two aunts, Pearl and Shandel were born. When we came in, he was seated and studying. He stood up, slowly. He embraced my father and when he turned around to me, I knew what was coming next; he was going to pinch my cheeks ... I was right. After a short conversation we left. Then we went to see my grandfather's property. He owned a couple of acres of farmland that he leased to a farmer. As we were walking I felt my shoes getting wet. I took them off—the water was ice cold.

"Why is this water so cold?"

"Pull out a carrot and eat it," my father said. I did and it was very sweet, but I didn't get the connection.

"We have an underground spring here." I still didn't get the connection.

"Will I be able to raise horses?"

"Maybe."

My two cousins, who were helping me at the market, were getting rich. Whatever money we made we divided in three equal amounts. When the market closed, I started to teach my two cousins and some other Hassidic boys how to play football, until my Uncle Yitzhak found out. He told them to go home and study their portion of the Chumash (The Five Books of Moses) for that week. Well, I didn't get away so easy either. After being rebuked, he was looking at my football. There was anger in his eyes, "You will kick this ball to the gutter and never touch it again!"

"This ball was my birthday present from my Uncle Moisho, my father's brother."

"You will do as I tell you, and then you will go to the mikvah and clean yourself, because this ball is made of pigskin. Make sure you grab my two sons because they have to go to the mikvah too. Before you enter the mikvah, you take off your clothes, wash yourself in the nude with the well water and then go into the mikvah."

"Uncle Yitzhak, you will not tell mother about the non-kosher football?"

"I will not tell her, but from now on, I would like to see you in Temple every Friday night."

I knew, and he knew, that this was blackmail but I could not start a revolution. A couple weeks later my Uncle Yitzhak brought me a kosher football.

Friday night I went to the Shul, but I never learned to pray as fast as the rest of the congregation. Before I was able to finish a quarter of a page, my two cousins had finished the whole page. As a matter of fact, they didn't need the prayer book with them; they had memorized the whole Friday night service! After a while I was looking forward to Fridays. After finishing all my work, I also went to the mikvah, and then returned home and changed my clothes for Shabbat.

# A Child's Last Vacation

As the sun was setting, there was a transformation going on among the Jews. The labors of the week came to an end, and all were ready to welcome Shabbat. Everybody in Kaminsk belonged to the Orthodox sect. All day my mother helped my Aunt Baila prepare food for the evening. On Friday we looked forward for the feast honoring the Queen of Shabbat. My Uncle Yitzhak came in, dressed in a black, wide-rimmed hat (Shtromel), a long, black silk unlined coat (Kapot), white socks and black shoes. I wore my best suit, a white shirt, a yarmulke and black shoes that were shining. I was ready to go to the Shul. My mother's eyes glowed with pride as she said, "You look like a Rabbi."

I also noticed a bright smile on my uncle's face. My two cousins were dressed the same, except for the skullcaps on their heads. We went outside and a throng of people going to the Shul met us. It was a beautiful sight to see men bedecked with shiny Kapitas and Shtroim. They went to the Rabbi's house to accompany him as a procession to the Schulte Temple. The Temple was packed. I don't remember whether the Shul had electricity or not.

When the service was finished and the people started to go home, you knew which houses were Jewish. Instead of the naphtha lamps, there were Shabbat candles. My uncle greeted everyone with "good Shabbat." We washed our hands and sat down at the table. My uncle said the prayer over the wine and the challah (braided bread). We all broke off a piece of the challah, recited the prayer over the bread and started to eat. After the meal, we all joined in prayers and songs of welcoming the Shabbat (Zimiris).

Shabbat was a day of prayer and study, but not for me. I had enough of prayers. I went to the shul, and when they started to read the Torah I used to sneak out. I went and picked up my cousin Reizel, and promised to show her what a river looked like. It was not a real river—it was just a running stream. I really enjoyed being with her, even when she was scared. Babysitting was not so bad after all. In Lódz, Reizel went to school around the corner from our house. Because the school was so near, she always joined us for lunch. For the first time, she asked me whether I liked girls. I avoided this question.

The summer was coming to an end and I was almost sorry we would have to leave the shtetl. I had been so busy I didn't have time to miss Lódz. I had gotten to know a lot of people. Many were pupils of my Grandfather Shloimo Vigdor. When they heard my name, they told me stories about him and what a good melamed he had been. At the same time, they started to praise my Uncle Yitzhak by saying that he should have been a rabbi.

When my father came to bring us home, he asked me if I would like to come back to Kaminsk some time. I told him I wanted to spend two weeks with my relatives in Belchatow. My mother's aunt, Hilda Haft, lived there, and they had horses. I also wanted to spend some time in Piotrkow with my Aunt Ruchel. I knew they had a fruit orchard and they also bred horses.

With some of the money I saved, I bought that little puppy dog, but it died four weeks later.

# Chapter 4

## A Time Ends and A Life Begins

I went back to school and once again I got Kmiecz, the anti-Semite, for my home teacher. The first assignment was to describe how we spent our vacations. I wrote about the Wednesday markets and how I worked and saved some money to buy a dog. I also wrote about the tannery and my hours spent watching the men working. I described how leather was transformed from the hides of cows. I described the Jewish life there and its differences from life in Lódz: how the water that came from the earth was clear and cold, there was no electricity, my father taught me to ride horses and my mother taught me to milk a goat. Once my mother was milking a cow and I asked who taught her. "You watch and then you try," she said. I explained how my mother and I went to pick mushrooms in the forest after a rain. I wrote as much as I could about the Jews, of their lives and the existence of the little shtetl called Kaminsk. For the first time in my life I got an A+ on my writing, but he was still an anti-Semite.

I always hated the month of March in Poland. The weather was never predicable. It rapidly changed from snow to rain and got windy. There was a Polish saying, "The month of March is like a cooking pot; one minute it is cold and the next minute it is hot." I could not wait for the March weather to draw to a close, and I was looking forward to June. Then I would be finished with the fifth grade, and Kmiecz, my anti-Semitic teacher. He didn't bother me, but he was brutal towards the other students in our class. He would use physical force for any class infringement. I could not understand why he hated Jews, and yet he spent most of the day teaching us. As a teacher he was not bad, as we were ahead of other classes. I guess we were afraid of him, and wouldn't dare not to do our homework.

I was an avid reader. One day a book fell out of my briefcase, and Mr. Kmiecz happened to pass by. He saw the title of the book, *The Idiot*, by the Russian writer Dostoyevsky. For a while there was a silence from both sides. He slowly picked up the book, and as he finished reading his piercing eyes were upon me. With a stern voice he said, "See me after school."

I was trembling from fear at the mere thought of what he was going to do to me. I thought I should run home and return with my father, but I knew that would be futile … he would be on Kmiecz's side. Inwardly I was angry. I had the right to read anything I wanted on my own time. I also knew that he had the power to make me repeat the fifth grade if he so desired. I was waiting for our class to finish, and when everyone left, I was still sitting at my desk. Maybe he forgot about me? I knew that I could not be that lucky. About a half-hour later he appeared smiling as he entered, and I stood up the way we always did when a teacher entered a room.

"Sit down!" he commanded me in his usual voice. He barked, "Are you a communist?"

"No, I belong to the Beitar."

"What is this, a Communist cell?"

"No," I told him in a stammering voice. "Beitar has nothing to do with Russia or Communism. Beitar is a Zionist organization, which will train young people for the harsh life in Palestine. Someday the Jews will have their own land." After I said it, my heart was beating and expecting the worst.

He looked at me and was quite puzzled. His eyes were sternly looking at me, but I didn't want to stop talking. The year before I had written about Kaminsk; this time I was describing Palestine.

"Your father fought for Polish independence and *you* want to leave Poland!" he yelled at me.

"No, I don't want to leave Poland, but Pan (Mr.) Kmiecz, you professed many times that you don't like Jews, and now Hitler is at our doorsteps propagandizing against us. What future do we have here?" He knew exactly what I meant.

"Go!" he shouted. As I turned around to leave, he kicked me in the buttocks.

I went home, into my hiding place underneath the table where my father kept bales of textiles. The mere thought of what Kmiecz was going to do to me brought tears to my eyes. An hour ago I stood up to Kmiecz, and now I was scared thinking what was going to happen? My mother bent over the table and asked me what I was doing. I decided to tell her what happened and begged her not to tell my father. In one way, this did not matter, because the events of the following autumn would end my school years. However, this was the present reality.

She bent over and touched me, and as she was wiping my tears away, she kept patting my hair and said, "You are going to be twelve years old. He is your teacher and you were disrespectful to him. Pan Kmiecz, like your father, fought for Polish independence, hates the Russians and doesn't want anything to do with Russia. He despises them. I started to read books to you when you were one year old, because when I read books, a window opened up for us. I was able to step out from my little shtetl and step up to the window of the world. Now I can see you looking for that window. Look and read, and a new horizon will open up for you too. Books are good, but you also must discriminate what is good writing from bad writing. Hitler wrote a book in Germany that was very popular. While millions of people in Germany are reading it, he is advocating the destruction of all the Jewish people." She paused for a moment ... "Should you buy this book?"

I still felt I was right, but I also knew if wanted to pass the fifth grade I would have to amend my ways. Even though my mother had scolded me, she was encouraging me. It reminded me of the first time she told me about the journey through a window, because of books.

One day, I suspected that my mother wanted to tell me that she was going to have a baby. Before she had a chance to tell me about her pregnancy, I declared that I was twelve years old and knew about the birds and the bees. I told her that she would have to get somebody else to look for the Bocian, because now I really knew about these things from my friends. We both had a good laugh.

On May 17, 1939, a baby girl was born. She was named Sarah Keila, after my grandmother who had just died in April, on Erev Passover, in Brooklyn. This was so my grandmother's name would not be forgotten.

# SECTION TWO

## *How Then Shall We Live*

i memorized his pain
plaintive songs messaged
a journey into death's eyes
racing nightmare
streets and shadows
in a dusk red sky
from a window where strange birds chatter
bursting ears
as strings gather and tighten
is there a resurrection from this endless night
death his companion
black prison of dreams
beauty in madness?
must i be reminded
mourns the oboe
recurring
recurring
end of time
he glanced at the broken mirror
while the emperor of death welcomed him
as he climbed a step less ladder
into the void

Untitled poem written by Norman Cohen after Victor spoke to Mrs.
Cohen Willard's 10H English class, at Amityville High School, in
April 2000.

# Chapter 5

## Black September

As the summer of 1939 was approaching, my father told me that everybody in Kaminsk remembered me, and that my Uncle Yitzhak would like me to come back for the following summer. I didn't go back to Kaminsk during that summer. I had to wait until 1996. This is because in September 1938, Hitler demanded that the Sudetenland, a part of Czechoslovakia, which had a large German population, should be annexed to Germany. The German grievance was that the local German populations were discriminated against and must be liberated and annexed to Germany.

British Prime Minister Chamberlain signed an agreement with Germany, which gave them the right to occupy Sudetenland in order to avoid further aggression. The pact was signed and Prime Minister Chamberlain went back to London, with a declaration of "Peace in our time." A couple of months later, to be exact, March 15, 1939, Czechoslovakia was swallowed by further German aggression, and Czechoslovakia ceased to exist. The dogs of war had been loosed, and Kaminsk, like any other area, prepared for the outcome.

In September 1939, Kaminsk had thousands of Polish troops stationed there. Germany demanded a corridor from Germany to the bi-national city of Danzig (Gdansk). Poland refused with the slogan: "We are not going to give one button from our uniform." A couple of days later German forces invaded Poland, and on the first day of the war Kaminsk was bombed to oblivion. The only building spared was the church. After a couple weeks of ferocious and incredibly brave fighting, Poland gave up their whole uniform.

This unexpected attack on Kaminsk caused many fatalities among the civilian population including my cousin, Shloimo Vigdor, who was the oldest son of my Uncle Yitzhak. Uncle Yitzhak had been drafted into the army, captured and later released. When he came to our house, nobody had the heart to tell him about the loss of his oldest son, who was the first person to die in Kaminsk. Because of this, he never spoke to us again. We wondered if we were right not to tell him. The whole family mourned for this wonderful young man who was a scholar. Uncle Yitzhak became the Elder of the town. As Elder of Kaminsk, my uncle, in his letters, describes the plight of Jews there. My uncle's name disappears from records in mid-1941, but my Aunt Beila and four of her children were still there. Yitzhak Wejnman and his wife Beila and their five children: Shloimo Vigdor, David, Sheindel, Dwoira, Eliazer; my mother's aunt Yita; my grandfather Manuel Brajtburg along with his children; and my three aunts: Shaindl, Pearl, Yochva and her husband Shmul and their three children, were my family who perished in the decimation of Kaminsk. There were others whom I befriended and who gave me love. By the end of 1941, Kaminsk became Jewless.

For me and other boys, the army barracks next to our building was a haven, because most of us climbed up on the roof and thought it would be a place to observe how a war was being fought. I told everyone how my father fought in the First World War and how the army licked the Germans and the Russians. After all, he was an officer in the cavalry and he was not afraid of anyone.

We heard that Germany was burning down temples, prosecuting Jews and sending some Jews to Poland. They were taking their possessions and persecuting them. Everyone walking the streets of Lódz was reading how Germany was continually barraging Poland, and how the Germans wanted the corridor to Danzig. Thank God that Poland refused the Germans. My mother didn't believe that the Germans, who experienced the previous war, were very polite or helpful to Jews all these years later. "People do not change so fast," she quipped.

My father was inducted back into the Polish cavalry and was sent for the protection of Warsaw, without having an opportunity to say goodbye. Within three days the Germans marched into Lódz and for the first time I saw what a German soldier looked like. We went to meet them on Piotrkowska Street to see what kind of animals would burn Jewish temples. I organized several of my friends because I thought that it was our obligation to find out what our enemy was like. I didn't tell my mother where we were going because I knew she wouldn't let me to go. Piotrkowska Street was packed with people and

German soldiers in pairs, sitting comfortably in their cars, with rifles neatly on each side of the car and waving to the people.

It seems odd, but I was admiring the soldiers for how clean and polished they looked and how they were waving to the crowds even though they were the enemy; it was impressive. Some in the crowd were raising their hands with the Nazi salute and some Polish people were throwing flowers. I started to cry. Who are these people? Are they Polish citizens? (Many may have been German-Poles, but there were anti-Semitic Poles as well). I was crying for my father who was fighting in Warsaw against the Germans. Lines of tanks were passing by and we saw lots of swastikas and I wondered if this parade would ever finish. I could not stop crying and thinking, "Is this Poland?"

A couple lines away I saw two boys who I had a fight with some months before. They were always trouble. They would hide and wait for me. One would go behind me while the other went in front and pushed me over so I would fall on my back. Now they were wearing black uniforms and the swastika on their arm. One of them pointed his knife, miming that he was going to cut my throat. I pointed to him and gestured that I would do likewise. I decided that if I ever saw him again I would choke him. At that point we ran home with tears in our eyes.

After about four weeks, the fighting in Warsaw was over and finally my father came back home. He looked like he had not slept or shaved since he left. My father went over to the bed, collapsed and fell into to a deep sleep. We all were standing around watching over him— realizing how skinny he looked. We tried to take off his coat. It was shredded as if he had been using it as a shield to protect himself from bullets, and we found some lodged in the coat.

From what I have learned, his cavalry unit and others, had been part of a retreat. After the fall of Warsaw, they went to the Romanian border along with Polish leadership to form a defense line. On September 17, the Red Army crossed the Polish border in the east, in fulfillment of the secret Nazi-Soviet Pact and ended any prospect of Poland's survival. Poles who could, fled across the border into Romania, and many subsequently reached the west and continued the war as the Free Polish Forces. Among them were many pilots, who were welcomed into the RAF. They took part in the Battle of Britain. Others, like my father, managed to make their way home.

Mother didn't allow anyone to wake my father up while he was sleeping, and chased us out. I hid and watched my mother gently washing my father with warm water. She washed his face, then the rest of his body without disturbing him. After three days he woke up.

The face of our city was changing rapidly. We were immediately annexed as part of the Warthgeau region of the Reich. We were the first city to become completely Germanized. Lódz was renamed Listmannstadt after a famous WWI general. All the factories and even small shops were Germanized, which meant they were taken over with no form of compensation. All the street names were changed to German ones. Very ill children, and others, were taken out of the hospitals and killed. Over the next year there was much illness, tuberculosis, starvation and death.

# Chapter 6

## Moving, Smuggling and Sawdust

*The Ghetto*

On February 8, 1940, the order was given to establish the ghetto. It was supposed to take one day—it took weeks. On April 1, the ghetto was officially closed, and it was sealed on May 1. The rest of the city was separated from us. The Jewish Council was set-up and Mordechai Rumkowski was chosen to be the Älteste (Elder of the Jews) of Lódz. In essence, he was the ruler of the ghetto, presiding over ghetto life. Many regarded him as a self-aggrandizing megalomaniac. He encouraged artists to memorialize him; he appeared to revel in power and sometimes he was referred to as "King of the Ghetto." At the same time, he saw himself as a fatherly savior, and some believe people lived longer because of his efforts.

## Moving Smuggling and Sawdust

April 1941 was when we were forced to move to Rybna 17 in the ghetto; 11 go Listopoda 58 would soon be nothing but a memory. Rybna 17 was our ghetto address from April 1941 until August 15, 1944 when the ghetto was dismantled. It was nearly one year since we were incarcerated in that filthy pitiful place called the ghetto.

We were luckier than most people. The building had three floors and a reservoir on the fourth floor. Most of the tenants living there were from before the war. The only dwelling left for us was a tiny step-down 7x8 room under the stairs. It had a small window from which we could see the cobblestones in the yard. We never saw the sunshine, but why was I complaining? Some families shared their tiny rooms with other families. It was a far cry from what we were used to living in. Some tenants thought we would be able to live like this for a short time because the war was supposed to last only six months; Germany would be defeated, and we would return to our own apartments. That was a great miscalculation. As far as I know, there are only two survivors, Morris Pinchewski and myself, from some twenty families who lived there until the ghetto was evacuated in August 1944.

In order to get this hole of an apartment, my mother was appointed to be the superintendent of the building, because she had a small child and couldn't leave her to go to work. My father secured this position for her through someone he knew before the war. We helped her out as much we could. Before my father and I left for work, we took care of the building. No matter how tired we children were when we came home from work, we played football and other games with all our free time. I remember the young German-Jewish girl who lived next to us. She had a little pug nose and spoke with a slight lisp.

Thanks to a neighbor, who was smuggling food into the ghetto—my father joined them—we were doing much better than others. But there were always risks. There were six people involved in this smuggling ring, including my father. The head of the ring was Hulko, who was a horse trader before the war—he was a sleazy sort with many arrests. During this time he had many connections with the Polish underground, which was not well organized in Lódz.

Among the laws in the ghetto were the curfews, which were enforced from 7:00 PM to 6:00 AM. Posted signs reminded you, "If you are caught between the curfew hours you will be shot. If smuggling from the outside of the ghetto … you will be shot on the spot. Anyone who is caught helping smugglers will be shot on the spot."

Normally at 3 A.M. my father opened the gate and let Hulko and the others back in the ghetto. My father got his cut on the spot. Sometime in May, the Gestapo came and arrested them. Each charge was punishable as a capital crime. My father was charged with participating in the crime of smuggling for opening the front gate during the curfew. They were handcuffed, and one at a time they were taken into a waiting truck. Before my father left, with permission of the Gestapo man, my father approached us and very slowly articulated his words, "There is nothing to worry about."

He was sentenced to nine months in jail. I don't know why they didn't have a trial to send him out of the ghetto. Why didn't they shoot him like anyone else caught smuggling? Somewhere, there must have been a bribe. The men he was involved with were professional criminals and could easily have had gold or other valuable currency stashed away somewhere. In 1996 when I visited Poland, I discovered records that confirmed these things.

Through those nine months I had to do everything possible to help my family. Many days I worked for sixteen hours and brought home bags of sawdust with wood hidden inside. Sometimes the bag was heavier than I was. We invited many children into our room so they could warm themselves up. The winter was severe, and by the time you woke up in the morning, the water was frozen.

# Chapter 7

## The Hardest Year Yet

*Eyes*

1942 was the hardest and darkest time of our three-year incarceration in the ghetto. People disappeared continuously, and we never heard of them again. Tuberculosis and starvation continued to take their toll. My position at work was upgraded, and every once in a while I received a special packet of food that subsidized our family's meager rations. I was still at the woodworking factory, which gave me the opportunity to continue to bring sawdust home for heating our small room during the winter.

By the end of August 1942, rumors, good and bad, started to circulate throughout the ghetto. The good rumors were that the Germans were having a hard time on the Russian front. The bad rumors were that more people would be resettled from the ghetto. We had heard those rumors before.

On September 4, 1942, the Nazi appointed Jew, Mordechai Chaim Rumkowski, Chairman of the Lódz Ghetto Judenrat (council), made an announcement. This was the result of a demand by the SS, to deliver 24,000-25,000 (sources vary) Jews under the age of ten, and over the age of 65, to the train station for resettlement within the next eight days. This was not his first address concerning deportations, but it was certainly the worst. I was at the place where Chaim Rumkowski made that fateful speech:

*A grievous blow has struck the ghetto. They are asking us to give up the best we possess - the children and the elderly. I was unworthy of having a child of my own, so I gave the best years of my life to children. I've lived and breathed with children, I never imagined I would be forced to deliver this sacrifice to the altar with my own hands. In my old age, I must stretch out my hands and beg: Brothers and sisters! Hand them over to me! Fathers and mothers: Give me your children! I had a suspicion something was going to befall us. I anticipated "something" and was always like a watchman: on guard to prevent it. But I was unsuccessful because I didn't know what was threatening us. The taking of the sick from the hospitals caught me completely by surprise. And I give you the best proof there is of this: I had my own nearest and dearest among them and I could do nothing for them! I thought that would be the end of it, that after that, they'd leave us in peace, the peace for which I long so much, for which I've always worked, which has been my goal. But something else, it turned out, was destined for us. Such is the fate of the Jews: always more suffering and always worse suffering, especially in times of war.*

*Yesterday afternoon, they gave me the order to send more than 20,000 Jews out of the ghetto, and if not - "We will do it!" So the question became, 'Should we take it upon ourselves, do it ourselves, or leave it to others to do?". Well, we - that is, I and my closest associates - thought first not about "How many will perish?" but "How many is it possible to save?" And we reached the conclusion that, however hard it would be for us, we should take the implementation of this order into our own hands. I must perform this difficult and bloody operation - I must cut off limbs in order to save the body itself. I must take children because, if not, others may be taken as well - God forbid.*

*I have no thought of consoling you today. Nor do I wish to calm you. I must lay bare your full anguish and pain. I come to you like a bandit, to take from you what you treasure most in your hearts! I have tried, using every possible means, to get the order revoked. I tried - when that proved to be impossible - to soften the order. Just yesterday, I ordered a list of children aged 9 - I wanted at least to save this one aged-group: the nine to 10 year olds. But I was not granted this concession. On only one point did I succeed: in saving the 10 year olds and up. Let this be a consolation to our profound grief.*

*There are, in the ghetto, many patients who can expect to live only a few days more, maybe a few weeks. I don't know if the idea is diabolical or not, but I must say it: "Give me the sick. In their place we can save the healthy."*

*I know how dear the sick are to any family, and particularly to Jews. However, when cruel demands are made, one has to weigh and measure: who shall, can and may be saved? And common sense dictates that the saved must be those who can be saved and those who have a chance of being rescued, not those who cannot be saved in any case ... We live in the ghetto, mind you. We live with so much restriction that we do not have enough even for the healthy, let alone for the sick. Each of us feeds the sick at the expense of our own health: we give our bread to the sick. We give them our meager ration of sugar, our little piece of meat. And what's the result? Not enough to cure the sick, and we ourselves become ill. Of course, such sacrifices are the most beautiful and noble. But there are times when one has to choose: sacrifice the sick, who haven't the slightest chance of recovery and who also may make others ill, or rescue the healthy.*

*I could not deliberate over this problem for long; I had to resolve it in favor of the healthy. In this spirit, I gave the appropriate instructions to the doctors, and they will be expected to deliver all incurable patients, so that the healthy, who want and are able to live, will be saved in their place.*

*I understand you, mothers; I see your tears, alright. I also feel what you feel in your hearts, you fathers who will have to go to work in the morning after your children have been taken from you, when just yesterday you were playing with your dear little ones. All this I know and feel. Since 4 o'clock yesterday, when I first found out about the order, I have been utterly broken. I share your pain. I suffer because of your anguish, and I don't know how I'll survive this - where I'll find the strength to do so.*

*I must tell you a secret: they requested 24,000 victims, 3000 a day for eight days. I succeeded in reducing the number to 20,000, but only on the condition that these be children under the age of 10. Children 10 and older are safe! Since the children and the aged together equal only some 13,000 souls, the gap will have to be filled with the sick.*

*I can barely speak. I am exhausted; I only want to tell you what I am asking of you: Help me carry out this action! I am trembling. I am afraid that others, God forbid, will do it themselves.*

*A broken Jew stands before you. Do not envy me. This is the most difficult of all orders I have ever had to carry out at any time. I reach out to you with my broken, trembling hands and beg: Give into my hands the victims! So that we can avoid having further victims, and a population of 100,000 Jews can be preserved! So, they promised me: If we deliver our victims by ourselves, there will be peace!!!*

*At this point in the speech the crowd begins shouting. Many cry out:*

*"We will not let the children go alone! We will all go!"*

*These are empty phrases!!! I don't have the strength to argue with you! If the authorities were to arrive, none of you would be shouting!*

*I understand what it means to tear off a part of the body. Yesterday, I begged on my knees, but it didn't work. From small villages with Jewish populations of 7000 to 8000, barely 1000 arrived here. So which is better? What do you want? That 80,000 to 90,000 Jews remain, or God forbid, that the whole population be annihilated?*

*You may judge as you please; my duty is to preserve the Jews who remain. I do not speak to hotheads! I speak to your reason and conscience. I have done and will continue doing everything possible to keep arms from appearing in the streets and blood from being shed. The order could not be undone; it could only be reduced. One needs the heart of a bandit to ask from you what I am asking. But put yourself in my place, think logically, and you'll reach the conclusion that I cannot proceed any other way. The part that can be saved is much larger than the part that must be given away!"*[16]

We all had heard Rumkowski speak on many occasions. For the first time I saw tears in the chairman's eyes, convincing me that he truly loved children. Rumkowski pleaded with us to turn the children and elders over to the Germans for the sake of saving the ghetto. They would be safe; the prevailing notion being that nothing was going to happen to them.

[16] "Chaim Mordechai Rumkowski," Holocaust Education & Archive Research Team, accessed July 16th, 2010, http://www.holocaustresearchproject.org/ghettos/rumkowski.html.

The SS and Jewish police proceeded to surround the hospitals and forcibly removed all the patients. It didn't matter if you were there for a check-up or seriously ill. The SS went through the list of patients. If anyone was missing, they had to report to their deportation center, or another member of the family would be taken in their place. Anyone who resisted was shot on the spot! Some jumped to their deaths. They were herded like cattle to various assembly points at two of the hospitals, and from there they were taken to the Radogoszcz railway station. We didn't know that they, and all the previously "resettled" people since January 16, 1942, were shipped to Chelmno. The killing camp was about 2 1/2 miles from Chelmno nad Nerem, which is 31 miles northwest of Lódz. Carbon monoxide was piped into the hermetically sealed cargo area of the killing vans; permanent gas chambers were not yet developed. All the Jews from five other communities had been sent there since December 7, 1941. Martin Gilbert writes:

> *On December 7, 1941, as the first seven hundred Jews were being deported to the death camp at Chelmno, Japanese aircraft attacked the United States Fleet at Pearl Harbor. Unknown at the time either to the Allies or to the Jews of Europe, Roosevelt's day that would 'live in infamy' was also the first day of the 'final solution'.[17]*

Panic set in the Ghetto. Everyone was asking, "Who is going to be next?" "Where are they going to send our children and the elderly?"

We started to look for a safe hiding place. We knew the building well and had several in mind. We had a difficult decision to make. Were we looking for a place for ourselves, or were we also going to try to save the rest of the children from our building? We went through several locations which were suitable for us, but not for more than ten to fifteen children. On the fourth floor there was a water tank. If we let the water out, we could hide a dozen children and their mothers. My

---

[17] Martin Gilbert, *The Holocaust:A History of The Jews of Europe During the Second World War* (NewYork: Henry Holt and Company, 1985), 240.

father agreed to this plan. However, we had seventeen children and we also needed to protect their mothers. I noticed that my father looked ill, and I suggested that he should also look for a safe place to hide. I never gave a thought about myself. I was fifteen years old. I had a special card from the commissar. It said I was essential for the production at the shop where I worked; why did I have to worry?

Another place we thought of looking was in the cellar. We went down to see whether we could build an extra wall to hide everyone. We looked everywhere for other alternatives. In the cellar there was a pumping station to supply water to the reservoir. There was a motor with a belt leading to the center of the yard. It turned a large wheel and was connected to the water pump, which pumped water to the reservoir tank. The opening where the belt was measured approximately 18 inches by 20 inches. Many times the belt broke. I used to repair it, but I never explored the tunnel. My father removed the belt, I crawled into the tunnel and immediately I knew this place might be a safe haven for concealing the children. Then I realized the tunnel was wide and long enough to accommodate all the children and their mothers. There was enough room in the tunnel to stand or sit down, and enough oxygen. We removed the motor and pushed the belt back into the tunnel to use it to conceal the opening. When the last person would be in the tunnel, our plan was to cover the opening with garbage. Knowing how important sanitation was to the Germans, we thought they would never come near the place. We got some blankets, sugar water and other provisions. We felt we were ready.

On September 5, everyone was told to stay in their apartments unless they were instructed otherwise. We were to wait until our building was ordered to come down to the yard for selections. My father urged me to go to the hiding place. I didn't because I was so sure that my papers would save me. I also wanted to be close to my father. For the first time, I saw my father kissing my mother and putting his arms around my sister and my brother. He held them close for a while. My sister Sarah was a beautiful child; she was three years old. We never had a problem with her. I watched her when she took her first steps. No matter how tired or moody I was, when she started to giggle, I forgot about everything; I helped to bring up this child. My brother Favel (in Polish we used to call him Felek) looked to me as his hero. When he reached the age of seven, I started to teach him how to read and write Polish. He was smarter than I was and very eager to learn.

I never saw my father display any emotion toward us before. I looked at him with new eyes. I was fifteen years old, I worked hard and he knew it. I carried more than my share to keep our family alive. I was afraid, not for myself, but for my father. We almost lost him twice: once at the beginning of the war when he was called up without notice, and in 1941 when he was incarcerated for smuggling food into the ghetto. My mother begged him to hide for the sake of his family, but without success. My father was tall with blond hair and blue eyes; he would be the right choice to be the spokesperson for the building. The Germans always liked to deal with a more Aryan looking person than a more ethnic looking Jew.

We were all waiting for the German officer to come and inspect us. I rubbed my cheeks to look nice and red, and I put some paper inside of my shoes to make me look taller. I was scared, but I knew I had to put up a front for the officer when he came. All the children and their mothers had been in the tunnel since eight o'clock. Everybody had their documents, and now, we all prayed for their safety. I was worried and hoped that the children would not start to cry. There were children from one to eleven years old. If there were any mishaps, we would lose them, their mothers and who knows what would have been the retribution for the rest of us.

Sometime before noon, an SS officer and about ten Jewish policemen were surrounding our building. The officer was young, tall, handsome and looked at us with contempt. With a very fixed gaze he slowly looked around. He must have heard our hearts beating, and with a loud, booming command asked, "Where are the children and the old Jews?" At that point my father approached the officer, with his hat in his hand, and looking straight at him said, "Sir, you are the second officer who came to inspect us today, and whoever was eligible was already taken away." For a while there was silence. He began to swear and then said, "You better not lie to me."

I did all I could to conceal how scared I was. If anyone said the wrong thing, my father would have been doomed. Even the Jewish policemen were nervous. I had a feeling that somebody was going to pay a price. The officer called over a Jewish policeman and told him not to let anybody leave. He took two soldiers with him who were waiting outside in the street and proceeded to look for hidden people. We all believed that we were in trouble. We looked at each other and you could see the fear on our faces. The officer was gone for about ten minutes. To us it was an eternity. The officer and the two soldiers came down, without finding anyone, and you could see the anger on his face. He turned, abruptly pointing his baton at the stairs leading down to the cellar and demanded, "What is over there?" My father replied that we stored the garbage there and that the garbage had not been picked up for the last two weeks. Once again the officer called over some Jewish policemen and told them to search the cellar. He was walking and looking at us like he was selecting his next victims. We were afraid that if the Jewish policemen would suspect anyone was there, they would report to the SS officer. They were just as scared for their lives as we were, and they had to protect their families because they were unaffected by the selection. The officer didn't trust the Jewish police and started to walk down into the cellar. It didn't take too long before we heard him swearing and shouting, "You are all filthy pigs!"

It worked. It was too dirty for him to venture further into the cellar. They were safe.

The SS officer told the Jewish policemen to line us up for his selection. Several of my friends were selected to go to the gate where there were Jewish policemen ready to escort them to the wagon waiting for them outside our building. I was trembling from fear knowing I had misjudged. The proclamation said that there would be resettlement of children up to ten years old, and elderly people of sixty-five and over. I thought because I was fifteen years old and had a special pass that I would be by-passed. My friends were the same age. When my turn came, I stood straight and I held my card. The officer took my pass and with a sadistic smile he threw it on the ground and pointed for me to go to the gate.

I tried to protest, but at the same time I saw him reaching for his revolver. I was not going to wait any longer, and I ran as fast as I could over to the policeman who took me to the wagon. But, as I was trying to get away from him, I heard him laughing. I guess I was his entertainment for the day. I could not believe what had happened to me, and at the same time I started to look around. I was not going to leave the ghetto to be resettled without my family. More people came on our wagon and the others were filling up rapidly. I made a decision to jump when the wagon turned the corner.

There was one German soldier in the third wagon behind us, with one Jewish policeman on each wagon guarding us. I felt the Jewish policeman had his hands full with other people on the wagon and would not leave the wagon to chase me. It happened exactly as I had hoped. I jumped, ran through the field and circled back toward our house. I waited until it was safe to return. I felt proud of myself that I actually outwitted them. I told myself that I would never trust Chaim Rumkowski or the Germans again.

When I walked into our apartment I saw my mother and my two siblings crying. My father came over and held me tightly against him. I never remembered him holding me and comforting me like that before. I felt uncomfortable and didn't know what the whole fuss was about. I knew that the Germans were not going to get me; how naive I was. On that day I grew up. I was no longer just a boy who dreamed of football, skating and horseback riding. I thought, "Maybe one day I will be free again, but from today on I have to be a man." Many weeks passed since September 5, and we all mourned the people who were resettled. We went back to work in the ghetto and life went on. We all were thankful that we weren't caught. When Yom Kippur came along, we prayed that maybe next year we would be free.

The Germans never got their 25,000 people and had to settle for only 15,000 victims. My aunt and many other mothers, dressed their children in their best, made sure that they had all their documents, kissed their children and turned them over to the German soldiers for safe-keeping because we were told, "The ghetto is not a place for rearing children."

None of the children or their mothers survived.

# Chapter 8

## Ghetto Life, Girls, Death and Praying

*Kaddish*

Thank God that once again we survived the winter. So many people died during the previous winter of 1942 from freezing and malnutrition; they had nothing left to fight with. Life in the ghetto was getting harsher … our hopes were starting to wane.

The war was supposed to have lasted a couple months; it was now 1943, the fourth year. People were continuously being sent out from the ghetto on the pretext that they were going to be resettled. The speeches of Chaim Rumkowski, chastising us for not working hard enough, were falling on deaf ears. We worked for ten hours a day and gave as much as we could, but it wasn't enough. Our rations were cut and we just didn't have the strength to work any harder. The Jewish police sometimes forgot that we were also Jews. Their cruelty was unexpected and at times unimaginable. Sometimes I thought that Chairman Chaim Rumkowski and his henchmen believed that the war would last forever. To me, they were on the borderline of being collaborators with the Germans.

Still, in the midst of all this tragedy and suffering, people were falling in love and getting married. What I could not understand was why they wanted to bring children into such a dismal world. In spite of all this chaos people in the ghetto established an underground trade school, a symphony and a theater. We prayed and observed our religion as it had been taught for thousands of years. Everyone tried to forget the dead and attempted to be happy with the fact that at least we managed to survive. We were just hoping for a better tomorrow.

My father's health continued to decline. He lost a lot of weight and his clothes were barely hanging on his body. He also started to miss work and slept more. Every once in a while I could sense that my father was looking at me like he was evaluating me. What scared me the most, was that sometimes he coughed up blood and limped on his right side where he had been wounded at the beginning of the war. My mother gave my father more food than his ration, but I guess it was not enough. My mother was a remarkable woman. She did miracles with stretching our rations and kept reminding me that I had to teach the children how to read and write. She never learned how to read Polish and most of the language that was spoken in our home was Yiddish. She was a master of Yiddish. I don't think they had a public school in Kaminsk. She always read books and we always were treated to a story before we went to sleep. That's why it was interesting that she learned Hebrew, to read the Scriptures, when she was five.

Most of the time we had Sunday's off. I was always enchanted as I listened to my father telling us about the First World War and now I was repeating those stories to Felek. How proud I was when I saw my father marching in his uniform on Polish Independence Day. The gleam in his blue eyes and smiling face said, "I am a Jew, and I am an officer in the Polish army."

Our yard was adjacent to one of the oldest cemeteries in Lódz. Every once in while I climbed over the brick fence to the other side. I found some peace there. Usually I would bring a book with me. From all the places in the city, a cemetery was where I found solace and solitude. When I read books, I found myself forgetting where I was; I was transported to where the story was. These were my "journeys through the window" as my mother had taught me. In the stories, there were lands where humans were treated the way they should be treated.

I was sixteen years old and I had never gone out with a girl. I was wondering what that was like. I had a crush on a girl whose name was Gisela. She lived in our building, but she didn't know that I even existed. Once she tried to converse with me, but my tongue got twisted and she walked away laughing. Within a couple months she and her parents were evacuated for resettlement in Germany. Later on we learned that they all perished in Chelmno.

Spring arrived. It brought some warmth and the green leaves on the trees were trying to talk to us, "Wake up and spread your wings." But our wings were hanging down next to our bodies with no strength left. We looked at the sun as a goddess of pleasure and the winter as the Devil. Within a couple of weeks I turned over the soil on my little plot and planted my first tomatoes. At this time, several of our former neighbors came to visit my father and reminisced about the pre-war times.

Sala Finkelstein had been a friend of mine since I was six years old. She heard that my father was sick and came to visit us. She was two years older than I was, and when I started to go to school she used to help me with my homework. I had not seen her for about three years and was surprised to see how she transformed from a scrawny freckle–faced girl of fifteen, to an eighteen-year old beautiful, young woman.

"How are you Shlomo?" Before I had a chance to answer, my mother chimed in.

"He is wonderful … a lot of women in our building would like to adopt him."

My face turned red. I tried to deny what was being said, but the more I talked the worse it got. I will never forget how both of them were laughing. After a while the laughter subsided and I was angry that I had become the object of their amusement. Sala turned around, took my hand and led me out to the yard and said, "Remember we never joke about people we don't like."

We talked for a while about what had been going on in the ghetto. She told me that she had to see somebody in the neighborhood and would visit next Sunday. Sala always was nice to me. I guess I was like the brother she never had. After that visit, I saw Sala occasionally and was always delighted to see her on Sundays, because most of the factories were closed—it was the one day in the week that we tried to live as normally as we could. Sala showed up one early Sunday afternoon.

"Can we go some where private?" she asked.

"Can you climb?"

She nodded and we went outside. I put a ladder against the wall and motioned to her to start climbing. She started to laugh, "If I climb first you are going to be able see what I am wearing under my dress." I never gave a thought to that, but it would have been nice. I found her waiting for me and we both sat down on a tombstone. She started crying.

"What's the matter Sala?"

I was surprised when she said, "I miss you, Motek, Moishe, the yard and the way we lived," and she continued reminiscing. "Remember how we all tried to teach your mother's chicken to fly?"

At this point we started to laugh and forgot all the chaos around us. The sun started to set and the curfew would begin in about an hour, so we decided to leave. She put her arms around me and kissed me on the lips. I knew I was blushing, and kissed her back, lightly. She gave a curious look and started to laugh. "Shlomo, one of these days I am going to teach you how to kiss."

I saw Sala one last time, but she didn't see me. I hid from her because I was dirty from the bag of sawdust I was carrying on the way home from work. After the war I tried to find her, but she was not on any lists of people who survived. Her name was Sala Finkelstein and she lived at 11 go Listopada 58.

The next day, around noon, my mother arrived at my place of work at the Tishler Resort and told the guard that it was imperative for her to see me. I was summoned to the Commissar, Mr. Terkeltaub. I was not surprised, because in the past he used to send me on errands to different factories. He looked very somber and advised me that my mother was waiting for me at the guardhouse. Mr. Terkeltaub gave me a permission slip to leave the factory and told me that if I needed anything, he would help.

I knew that my father had not been feeling well for the last couple of days and I surmised that he might have to go to the hospital. I met my mother at the guardhouse and we hurried home. On the way home my mother told me that my father hadn't gone to work; he was too sick. It didn't take long before we arrived home and found him sleeping. I walked over to him, took his hand and asked how he felt; he gave me a slight squeeze on the palm of my hand. For the first time it dawned on me that my father was dying. How was this possible ... he had only lost some weight, and for the last couple of months there were some traces of blood in his phlegm?

My mother brought over some soup and told me to feed him. I propped him up, took a spoonful of soup and put it to his lips. He gently pushed it away. I was afraid if I forced it into his mouth he might gag. Once again I was holding his hand and felt the squeeze. I looked at my mother, and she motioned me to sit there and hold his hand. I looked at him. Here was a man who had been so full of life. He loved to ride horses, swim and tell stories from the First World War. He served in the Polish cavalry and was wounded at Tarnepole near the Ukrainian border. For that he received a medal for valor. What I could not understand was that his medal stated that he served from 1918-1921. In 1918 he would have been only sixteen years old. We had a picture of him sitting in full uniform on a cavalry horse hanging on the wall. How proud and handsome he looked. I was sitting there and my father was dying. He was losing his battle for life at forty-one, and at sixteen I was fighting for my life. I felt him loosen his hand; I tried to feel if there was a pulse ... his hand became waxy. I tried to talk to him and then I looked at my mother; she was sobbing. She took me in her arms and quietly said, "Now you will have to say Kaddish for a whole year."

I sat there motionless, just looking at my father and thinking, "Is this all of what life is?" Just minutes ago he was squeezing my hand, and now he was sleeping with the eternal sleep. I shivered even though it was June. The shiver was fear and I thought, "How dare you die ... why did you give up?" I kept looking at him as I was trying to transmit my thoughts to him. I took his hand and held it, looking at his face. His face was pale and rigid, his eyes and cheeks were sunken and the outline of a skeletal head was all that was left. My father died on June 18, 1943 at the age of 41. His suffering was over; we had to survive.

Within a couple of hours some men came to our house. They laid my father on a portable table, washed him and put the tachrichim (linen burial shroud) and his talit (prayer shawl) on him. He was ready to be buried. They positioned him so that that his legs were facing the door. The sunset was on the horizon and my mother lit the candle to welcome the Sabbath.

Somebody had notified my place of work, because it was Mr. Terkeltaub who had sent over the burial boards with a permission note to stay home for the coming week. The next day my father was buried at Marshinsky Cemetery in plot number 512. At the grave I said Kaddish for the first time. All of our family in the ghetto attended, including my father's brother Moisho, his wife Ruchel and many others. My uncle Moisho came over to me, put his arms around me and said, "You have to take care of my brother's family, and if you need any help come to me." I kissed him for the first time because I felt lonely.

I said Kaddish until January 1944 and then stopped. When my mother noticed that I no longer said Kaddish, she asked me why. I told her, "When you say Kaddish you are glorifying God and not the person who died. I will pray for my father in my own way." After that I refrained from saying Kaddish and the Ulainu, because I had to bow my head to the Almighty. God provided manna in the wilderness ... why couldn't He give us food in the ghetto?

# Chapter 9

## Resettlement and Goodbyes

*Felek and Victor*                    *Chava, Victor and David*

By mid July, rumors were circulating that the Ghetto was going to be resettled again. Over the past five years, the Germans had demanded that the Judanrat hand over people to work outside the ghetto. They would separate out more people and everything else would stay the way it had been. Compared to other years, 1943 was quite a peaceful year. That would change by June 1944, when another order of resettlement was given—10,000 more people were required. In the past, Rumkowski bargained down to slightly over 7,000 people and everything went back to normal.

Usually, some of the people were notified of resettlement and their ration cards were withdrawn. Afterwards they would report to the railroad station, were sent out and never heard from again. We never thought that anything would happen to them other than going to work outside the ghetto. After the ghetto went through a "cleansing", those who were left went back to work. Then we got new arrivals from other parts of Europe, who were shipped in to fill the void in the labor market.

When the ghetto was isolated from the rest of the city in April 1940, the population was approximately 160,000. Now our total population was down to 75,000 including women and children who were not able to work. We were at the lowest count ever.

Mr. Terkeltaub, my commissar, and I were always on good terms. The door to his office was always open to me. He had selected me to be a runner. When a German commission came to the ghetto to inspect our factories, their first stop was at the metal factory. We were told when there would be an inspection and he made sure that I would be there. When the inspectors showed up, I picked up a couple of sharpened saws and went back to our factory to notify Mr. Terkeltaub that the inspectors would be there within an hour. Of course, this gave us time to prepare materials and to show how efficient we were. I met him by chance on the street outside the factory.

"Mr. Terkeltaub, what is happening with the rumors about the disbanding of the ghetto?" "Are they true?"

"Yes. Beginning in August we are going to dismantle the factory and ship all the equipment to Germany."

I asked him one more question. "Are we going to go with the factory to Germany?"

"Victor, don't believe what they are saying. Hide yourself and your family because the Russian liberation will be here soon, and more than that I cannot tell you." I was astounded at his frank answer.

I went home and told my mother to get the family together. On the next Sunday, my aunts Sheindle and Regina, and my uncle Moshe assembled in our house. I told them what Mr. Terkeltaub had told me. Each of our families had small children, and the total, with the adults, was eleven. My aunt Sheindle said that she had the ideal place for our hiding place. All of us went over to her apartment and after removing a couple of boards we saw there was a large cellar. I voiced my opinion that the Germans will look for cellars.

"Climb down and remove the metal plate, and you will see a sub-cellar. The people who lived here previously used to store perishable food in there," my aunt Sheindle said.

I removed the metal plate and my uncle Moshe and I climbed down, lit a candle and carefully started to inspect the large underground pit. We noticed that there were free standing shelves. My uncle suggested that we dismantle the shelves and build a floor so we could bring down some bedding. We were standing about twelve feet below the floor level, and there was a cold and musty smell. "Well, my uncle said, we have a job to do to prepare ourselves before we send anybody down."

We needed food for at least five days. By that time the SS would have passed through our area. We all thought that this was only another resettlement, and after the beast had his bellyful, like in the past, we would return to work. We were very wrong.

The Germans started to divide the ghetto into sections, and new curfews were established. On all the streets, every resident had to report to the railroad station for the purpose of resettlement. We had just enough time to get to my aunt's building. She was waiting for us. The sub-cellar was ready and we practiced to see how fast we could run down and slide the hatch over the opening of the sub-basement.

My uncle Moshe and his wife didn't show up and this worried me. We were able to get the eight people down into the hiding place in less than two minutes … that was good. I decided to test it out myself, and told everyone to watch out for me. I walked out, and within a couple of minutes I returned … the room was empty. I pretended that I was looking for them and it didn't take me too long to spot where the opening was to the basement. I lifted the three boards and tried to see if a German would have noticed the sub-basement. I called for everyone to come out because it seemed that I had missed something. To be honest, I felt like a big shot, because everyone was listening to me.

"That plate which covers the sub-basement has to be camouflaged." I was thinking how clean the Germans were and what might prevent them from looking any further.

My mother said, "Of course! We are going to set the stage for whoever is going to look down there. Take an old straw mattress and put it over the plate. We have to set it up to look like somebody is sleeping on it because they are sick."

We brought down a mattress and some blankets. We also took some old medicines and put them on a wooden box next to the mattress. Then we found a candle and lit it until it was half burnt down. Then we extinguished it. I lay down on the mattress to leave an impression that looked like someone had been sleeping there. The women left and some of us urinated on the mattress to create a sickening smell.

During the next couple of days we were watching for our turn to be told to report to the station. Then the round up started. As soon we spotted the German SS with the Jewish police approaching our area, we hid in the pit. We were wondering why they didn't search the building we were in. We didn't have to wait long; within two days the area was bristling with Germans and Jewish police. They went through every apartment, knocked on the walls and looked for hidden places. All of us were holding our breath, including the children. In that pit, we were hiding my aunt Shindal and her daughter Reizel, who was 15 years old. There was also my aunt Regina with her 3-year-old son, who also was named after my grandfather Shloimo Vigdor. Finally, there was our family: my mother, my sister Sara Kaila, my brother Felek and myself. I don't remember whether my uncle Moshe and his wife ever showed up.

The under ground pit was cold and wet. After a while it really affected you. The worst thing was, we only had food left to last two more days Then we heard them opening the floor and the light was shining; we heard them swearing like we expected, and they left. We didn't dare leave our hiding place for fear of getting caught.

As the days passed, the children were getting sick and the adults were suffering from coughing. It had been four days and the inspections by the SS didn't subside. My mother turned to me and said, whispering, "I don't think we have a choice. Sarah is very sick, and if we don't give up she will most probably die." We all climbed out. It was already dark, but we didn't dare light a candle for fear that somebody might spot us. Sarah definitely had a fever and her face had a yellowish hue. Mother said to the others, "Sarah is sick, therefore tomorrow we are going to give ourselves up. They promised that we are going to Germany and they need our labor. The war is coming to an end and they let us live for five years, so why would they want to kill us now. We will not divulge your hiding place—you will be safe." I was hoping that one of the others would try to stop us, but it would not have mattered—there was really no other choice for us. Sarah was sick and we had to get help for her. I saw pain and fear in their faces. I knew they were willing to share everything that was left, but they knew they could *not* stop us. The next day we gave ourselves up.

A German SS encountered us and asked us where the others were. We told him that there were no others. He looked at Sarah and told the Jewish Police Officer, "Escort them to the railroad. When you get there, let the doctor look at this poor child."

It was obvious that we were not the only ones who came to the conclusion that it was safe to leave the ghetto. When we arrived at the station there were several columns of people to be loaded on the trains. Everyone had a look of uncertainty of what was going to happen next. There was that unfocused stare of confusion.

The Jewish policeman escorted us to a hut, which had a Red Cross marking on it. A doctor came out wearing a white gown and looked at Sarah. He went back in and came out carrying a cup. The doctor gave some milk and honey to Sarah, and she eagerly drank it all down. I thanked the doctor for his help. He interrupted me, "When you get to the destination you are going to, make sure this young child sees a doctor." Once again I tried to thank him, but he dismissed my gesture. "Stay in the line, go on to the train and don't forget what I told you. Now get on the train."

I almost felt grateful to him. Maybe there were some nice Germans. Maybe it was because he was a doctor. I looked at Sarah and some color was back in her face. She weakly smiled at me. As always, that brought a smile to my face. I took her from mother; she was beautiful and helpless. She had beautiful blue eyes and curly blonde hair. Yes, she definitely was a Breitburg.

## Goodbye Lódz : August 15, 1944

We joined the line to get on the train. As our turn came, we each received a loaf of bread. Jewish policemen assisted my mother up into the train. Once mother and Sara were in, Felek and I climbed aboard. It took awhile until the train was filled up, and then I heard the door slam and a latch locked us in. I looked around and tried to count how many people were on the train. I was surprised. When I finished counting there were only sixty people. We must have been the last train loaded, because we had a little more space than the people in the other trains. We didn't move for about two hours. Then the train slowly started to go forward. Goodbye Lódz. I felt that we would never come back once we entered Germany. In a matter of minutes, Lódz was behind us. There was a great silence. We feared what was ahead of us. I thought, "After the war, we will try to go to America."

The officers promised us that we were going to Germany because factories were there, and they needed us as workers. It made sense, because for the last four years we produced whatever their army needed. Lódz was so well organized that we felt we were indispensable to the Germans. We made the shoes, socks, pants, sweaters and shirts for their uniforms. But even with feeling so sure of ourselves and believing we were needed, we wanted to do something more than just be their workers. What they didn't know was that we could have produced twice as much as we did. At times we did some deliberate work slowdowns. That was about our only organized resistance in Lódz; the last ghetto to be disbanded. We were convinced that this journey was only a resettlement and we would have to start all over again somewhere. Somebody on the train asked that we all pray for our safe arrival. Everybody stood up, and prayer reverberated throughout the train. It wasn't as much a formal prayer as it was a plea to God for mercy for his children of Israel, and for our deliverance to safety. The train began to pick up speed. We were wondering where in Germany we were going. We must have been traveling for several hours, with some stops to permit other trains to pass. We observed that eastbound trains were army trains and westbound trains were transports for the Red Cross. We knew that the Germans were suffering heavy casualties on the eastern front. Were they losing the war? Were they winning on the western front? Is this why they needed our help?

We stopped for the night and every one settled down to sleep. We still had bread and there was a barrel of water. If we had to go to the toilet, we put up a little curtain and went through a crack in the floor as we relieved ourselves down onto the railroad tracks. The mood on the train improved. Most were thinking that if they wanted to kill us, why would they use such a valuable train? We must have stopped a dozen times. Every time we stopped, we stood there for hours. This was the third day.

All of sudden there was a commotion. We went through a gate and the train stopped. There was silence, and we knew we had arrived. Everyone put on their backpacks and waited for the doors of the train to open. I heard my heart beating. I was not at ease and my lips were trembling. My mother gathered us in her arms and told us to stay together. "If for some reason we get separated, we should not forget that our meeting destination is with my sister in Brooklyn." She kissed us. I hugged my mother.

I said, "Nothing is going happen to us, we are going to stay together."

I took Felek's hand, but he pulled it away and said, "Take care of Sarah. I am twelve years old and am able to help myself." I smiled at him. He certainly was growing up. I was surprised at his reaction. He turned out to be such a good-looking kid. He was a Breitburg; blond and blue eyed. I am a cross breed between the Wajnmans and Brajtburgs.

Waiting for the door to slide open was hard. We didn't know what to expect. At that moment I felt we should pray to the Almighty, "Please let this nightmare end for us so that one day we might go to the Promised Land and serve you for eternity."

# SECTION THREE

*By The Rivers of Babylon*
*We Sadly Hung There Our Harps*

Excerpt from the play, *Chagrined* ©Joseph G. Krygier 2012

The Germans were meticulous in labeling us. Jews, Catholics, Evangelical Protestants or Christians, Roma, homosexuals and political prisoners, each with their own sewn on identification symbol.

Wladek was a Christian, and he responded to the questions and doubts of the others in the barrack about the officer's reason for speaking to us the way he did.

Shall I take the good and not the evil?

They can kill our bodies ... we all have to die anyway. We accept the inevitability of death. Why should it be any different now? I realize that among us exists many views about what may or may not happen after that, but this I know ... These Nazis cannot rob me of my soul. This is my defiance. They cannot rob me of what God gave me that will live beyond this body. And when I am judged by God, I pray that my life will have been lived in the balance to have been more helpful to others than to myself, because I also believe what the young Jewish prince and prophet Daniel wrote, when he was in captivity by the most ruthless men on earth at that time:

"And many of them that sleep in the dust of the earth shall awake, some to everlasting life and some to reproaches and everlasting abhorrence."

So ... you can take it or leave it. This is what I believe. Their tyranny over my body will not be tyranny over my soul.

Two days later, Wladek attempted to give aid to a very weak man on our work detail. A Jewish Kapo beat him to death with his whip handle for disregarding his order to leave the man alone.

Let me ask you something ... if even for one moment you could do something to change the world, would you do it for yourself or for others? We cannot allow fear, to cause logic, reason or even faith to lose their place in our lives. Fear can consume all of these. Fear is what made so many simply refuse to live anymore; it was easier to die.

# Chapter 10

## Chimneys, Tears and Surviving

*Pyramid*

Abruptly the door slid open, and the men in prison uniforms shouted, "Out of the train now!" "Make it fast!" We hurried off the train. I looked around and saw that the S.S., with their dogs, surrounded us. I was not so sure that we were in Germany. A chill went through my body, "What is happening?" The words were on my lips, but not spoken.

"Women and children to the right and men to the left!" was the next command.

I decided to stay with the family; I was only seventeen, I wasn't a man.

"Go with the men. I will take care of the children," mother said.

"But we promised each other that we were going to stay together. I want to go with you," I begged.

"No, you have to go with the men … please … go."

Before I had a chance to answer, a man grabbed me by my arm and pushed me towards the column where the men were.

"Listen to your mother and go with the men," his voice boomed.

"Who is he to tell me where to go?" I thought.

I turned around … I didn't see my mother or my siblings.

"All right," I thought. "For now I will go with the men, but the minute I am settled I will find them. There are too many people to fight now, but nothing will stop me from finding them."

"Move fast, move fast," the SS repeatedly screamed at us.

The men in stripes were also screaming at us. Whistles were blowing, dogs were barking, men were pushing; I didn't know where to move. It reminded me of a cattle round up in the cowboy movies. Many voices were shouting, "Why are they all screaming at us?" "What is happening here?" "Are we walking into a trap?"

My mind was racing in every direction. I was looking to escape, but the SS and their dogs had us corralled. I found myself in front of a German officer. He wore a black uniform with a brown shirt with the SS insignia. He pointed a horsewhip at me and motioned that I should go to the left. I was like a robot. There was no more arguing or thinking … just obeying and doing precisely what I was commanded to do. I ran to the building where the other men were assembled.

"Take your clothes off and hang them up. Your clothes have to be disinfected!" was the next order that was shouted. "You're going to be inspected and afterwards you are going to take a shower."

I never gave any thought as to how we were going to get our clothes back. We were told that our clothes had to be tagged with our names, and after the shower we would get them back. We lined up for the inspection. An SS officer was pointing to each person indicating that he should go to the right or to the left. When my turn came, he pointed to the left. I hesitated for a moment and thought, "Maybe I should go to the right? All the people being selected to go to the right look sickly, and most will probably wind up in the family compound."

A man who was next to me fainted. Without a thought, I bent over to pick him up. The SS officer directed me to help the man to the adjacent room on the right. I walked in with him, set him down on the floor, walked out of the room and went to my place in the line on the left. Within in a couple of minutes the door to that room was closed. Had I remained in there a few seconds longer, I would have been locked in and killed.

Again the SS officer pointed at me, motioning for me to go to the left.

"Mach du schnel (make it fast)," he barked at me.

This time I moved to the room where there were showerheads coming from the ceiling. Within minutes the room was filled with the rest of the selected men. We were waiting for the water to come on. The doors were closed, and we were standing naked in total darkness … waiting. It seemed like an eternity.

"They are going to kill us," somebody shouted. "They are playing a game with us," someone else said, trying to sound comforting.

Again the doors opened up, some more people came in, the doors closed and this time the water came down from the showerheads. We all felt relieved as we washed ourselves in total darkness. It wasn't long until the doors opened up. Camp inmates in striped uniforms were standing there, holding sticks. They yelled at us, "Get out … fast! Another group is coming in."

As we ran by them, they kept hitting us and swearing at us. I was too fast for them to be hit, but many had red marks all over their bodies. I could not understand all this brutality from other inmates. I came over to a long table where there were piles of clothes. Some other inmates were there; they looked at you, and threw some clothes at you. I grabbed a pair of pants, a jacket and a pair of shoes. The pants were slightly too long, the jacket was fine, but the shoes were tight. I went over to one of them and politely asked if I could exchange the shoes.

"Get away you Jew," he said in Polish.

I stood up to him. "You should know better," I said, while looking him in the eyes. For a while there was a stand off.

A German soldier approached us. "Vas is los" (What is the matter)?

Before the Polish inmate had a chance to say anything I spoke, "How am I supposed to work with these shoes when I can't even put my feet in them? Am I supposed to cut off my toes?" I must have looked funny. I was standing, holding my up pants with one hand, wearing a jacket and holding a pair of shoes that anyone could have seen were too small.

"Go over to the pile and pick up a pair of shoes." I immediately thanked him; he also pointed where the pants were. "Go and exchange those stupid pants." Like lighting, I was on the top of the pile of pants and I picked the best I could find.

The German looked at the Polish inmate with the same hatred as if he were a Jew. I knew that somehow I had to make peace with the Pole. While he was handing out clothes I approached him.

"What do you want now?"

"I want to apologize for the misunderstanding."

"You've got guts," he said smiling. I reached out and we shook hands. To tell the truth, I was scared about the consequences, but with my apology, and shaking his hand, I felt the crisis had passed.

They herded us into a wooden barrack. On each side there were rows of bunks, three levels high. After all us were inside, a whistle blew. We were told to line up on each side. A tall heavy-set man, with a whip in his hand, came in and looked around.

"I am the Kapo of this barrack. What I am going to tell you I will only repeat once: You are shit! You are vermin, a cockroach and an ant. If you don't want to die, you better do what I tell you. I don't care if you live or die. In the morning you will hear a whistle. You will get up and wash yourselves. You are going to get some bread and a piece of margarine. When you hear another whistle you will step outside. When you get out there you are going to stay in three rows with your hats on. When the German officer comes over to our barrack, you will hear my order, "Hats off," and all of you will take your hats off at the same time … understood? You are going to be counted. We call this an Apel. Now you are going to practice, all of you, taking the hats off at the same time. Later when you hear the whistle, you will step outside for the Apel."

The Apel was called and we stood at attention until we were counted. By then we were totally exhausted. We had not eaten since the evening before and now we were standing in line for our supper. Each of us got a round deep metal plate, and we were told to keep it. One of the camp trustees poured in some watery soup with three pieces of potatoes floating on top. I was assigned, with five young boys to sleep on the top part of the bunk. There were some blankets there. I was the first one to go up and I grabbed one, covered myself and was soon fast asleep.

A sharp whistle awoke me from my sleep.

"Out of the beds and get outside for the Apel," the Kapo screamed.

I didn't need to get dressed, because I had fallen asleep with my clothes on.

I asked, "Where is the latrine? Is there any water to wash with?"

I was directed to go to another barrack two buildings away. It didn't take long before I was ready. We were standing to be inspected and counted. Even though it was August, it felt chilly. I wondered, "Where are we? Are we somewhere in North Germany?" I don't remember how long we were standing for the Apel. All I remember is that the sunrise of a new day appeared in the sky. It must have been about five o'clock in the morning because of where the sun was.

Once again we got a slice of bread, a piece of margarine and some kind of liquid to drink. I didn't dare ask if that was all we were going to eat until the evening. We were given the freedom to walk around, but we were told not to approach the electric fences. I walked outside, and for the first time I tried to evaluate where we were.

There were two rows of concrete posts that were spaced approximately ten to fifteen feet apart. Eight rows of barbed wire were strung. Each wire was fastened to a china holder. There were elevated posts with strobe lights, and each post had two SS soldiers with revolving machine guns. Each post was within visual range of the others. Signs warned that the wires were electrified, and any one approaching the fences would be shot. There was no way anybody could escape from this place.

I said to myself, "What are we doing here? Whatever is going on here I have to find out where they keep the women and children." No matter which trustee I asked, no one could give me an answer. This went on for a while until a man stopped in our barrack and inquired about a particular person.

"Are you from Lódz?"

"Yes, I am looking for my son. This is the last barrack left, then … " He didn't finish his sentence.

"Can you tell me, where are the women and children's barracks?" I felt that I had caught him by surprise.

"Did you come yesterday with the transport from Lódz?"

"Yes, I came with my mother, my twelve year old brother and a four and half year old sister."

This time I saw his face soften up and he had tears in his eyes.

"Come here. Do you see the smoke above the barracks?" I began to respond.

"Don't answer me, just listen to me. One hour after you arrived they were all gassed and cremated. My son was on that train, too." He just turned away from me still murmuring, "They are all dead." All I could comprehend was the word dead. "It's impossible," I thought. "He wants to scare me. They promised us we were good workers and they needed us. Maybe his son is dead, but not my family." The Lódz Ghetto had possibly been more isolated from outside information that any other in Poland. When the early deportations were taking place, we had no idea that the people were going to Chelmno to be executed. Based on our production of necessary war supplies for the German Army, many thought we were indispensable. Now, the reality of what had been going on struck me. I tried to find some hope, but to no avail. I was trying to fool myself with false hope.

I ran to the barrack to ask the Kapo if what this man had said was true. As I entered the barrack and looked at the other inmates, I knew the man had told me the truth. All I wanted to do was find a place to think, and when I found it, I just could not sit. I had promised my father that if something happened to him I would protect the family. Why did I give in to my mother to leave the hiding place? Would we have been better off if we had all been killed together? Why did she push me away to go with the men? At that point I spoke to God, "Why did you spare me? Please take me. I don't care if I live." I don't remember what happened for the next couple of days until a man spoke to me.

"If you die, then Hitler will succeed. Therefore, you have no choice but to live. Maybe somebody is alive. Don't say Kaddish yet." I thought, "Yes, he is right. I will refuse to say Kaddish until I find a witness who saw them die." I grieved for them, but now I wanted to live. I thought, "The man is right and I must thank him, I have to survive." I looked for the man, but I never found him again.

For a while we didn't work and that gave us more time to mourn, but the nights were the most awful times. In the darkness of the night you could hear sobs all around. Sometimes I climbed down from my bunk, found one or two people and tried to console them. I tried to give them some false hope that maybe not all of them had perished. "Don't say Kaddish yet. We all have to pull ourselves together and look good just in case there will be another selection."

Within a week there was another selection. All the young boys, my age and a little younger, were told to assemble in front of the barracks. There were three rows, approximately 150-200 standing at attention waiting for a selection. Were we going to be selected to go to work? Or were we being selected for the gas chamber? No matter what they were going to tell me, I was not going to believe them any more.

We were brought to attention and heard the command, "Hats off!" and our hats came off in unison. A tall, lanky SS officer with a medical insignia was looking us over with a slight smile. This time I stood erect, looking at him straight in the eyes. After a while, with his hand pointing at the first person, he started the selection. This time we were told to step forward. He selected approximately fifty boys and the rest were dismissed.

"You were selected to work. You will be treated better and you will be getting better food." That sounded familiar. Didn't the doctor at the Lódz station say that as soon as we arrived at our destination we should seek medical help for Sara? Did she get it? Now the Germans were going to treat us better? I didn't believe a word he said.

"Follow me," he commanded. We came to a barrack and were told to line up in a single line. As I entered, there were three inmates at a table. "Tell me your first name, last name, date of birth and where you came from?" After I gave him all the information, he turned me over to the next inmate. "Put out your left arm!" he commanded. He grabbed my arm and twisted it until the back of my arm was facing him. I was not able to see what he was doing, but I was able to feel that a needle was pricking my skin. "Your number is B7568," said inmate #2. I looked at the back of my lower arm and there was a tattoo, B7568.

Someone motioned for me to go to inmate #3. "Sit down and don't move." At this point, inmate #3 grabbed my head and began to cut off all my hair. "Now you are ready to take a shower—get going." I could not help myself and I quipped back at him, "That will have to wait until I have my dinner." For the first time I heard somebody laugh, and so did I.

After the shower each of us got a uniform with some patches. "You have to sew them on the right side of your jacket. The number patch goes on top, the red triangle with the point facing to the bottom and the yellow point facing up." There weren't any explanations given to us as to the meaning of the patches, but we soon we found out by ourselves that the red meant we were communists and of course, the yellow meant we were Jews—as if I needed to be reminded.

To our surprise, we got a pair of socks and a pair of underwear. I retained my shoes. I didn't want to go through another hassle. We dressed ourselves and looked quite decent. The pants and the jacket fit pretty well. We also got something that looked like a beret. I started to laugh and said, "We look like prisoners from the American movies." Every part of our clothes had white and dark blue stripes running vertically.

We were taken outside and marched for some time until we came to a gate; we were turned over to an officer, with two other camp inmates who were waiting for us. I noticed that on the gate there was a sign:

# "Arbeit Macht Frei" : Auschwitz

They marched us over to a two-story red brick building. We walked up to the second floor, and to our amazement we saw rows of three high single bunk beds. Each bed had a blanket neatly tucked in under a straw mattress. The floor and room were clean and it even had windows. Some were open.

The Kapo said, "This is Block 12 and you are going to stay here for a while. Here are the rows of bunks and you better remember to keep things as clean as you see them now. I am the Kapo of this building; I have a whip! If you don't want to meet my whip, just obey my orders. Here are some needles and cotton. Make sure that you sew on your patches and make them perfect. When you hear the whistle, make sure you walk down for the Apel. Remember … I don't take any nonsense!"

After the Apel, we met some of the old timers who built the buildings in 1940. We were warmly welcomed, and what surprised me was that there were so many Catholics among them.

During the day all we did was clean whatever we were given. At night it was a different story. The horrors we experienced were getting worse. I sometimes lay half awake in the middle of the night, talking and fighting with my mother. I kept repeating the same sentence, "I want to go with you." Usually, one of the boys helped me get back to sleep. After two weeks we were divided and were told that we were being sent to a different labor camp. Once again we were faced with the fear of the unknown.

# Chapter 11

## Horses, Ashes and Pigs

*Shoes*

From June 1942 to January of 1945, Budy, an enclave of Auschwitz, was an agricultural labor camp on an SS farm located about four kilometers from the main camp. The first laborers dug ditches, cleaned and deepened fishponds; then it became an agricultural labor camp. At various times there were up to 400 Jewish, Ukranian and Polish women prisoners there. One of the most infamous atrocities at this camp was the slaughter of Jewesses by female German guards.

When I was moved to Budy there were two barracks, which housed about two hundred inmates in each. Hungarians occupied one, and the other one had a mixture of political prisoners: Catholics, Christians, Polish and Greek Jews among others.

We came late in the afternoon and were taken to one of the two barracks. We were met by the Kapo and put through the usual ritual. We were told the camp rules and what was expected of us. However, there were no threats like in the prior camps. He spoke to us in German and explained that we were going to be divided and assigned to different work details. I noticed that he had a red-green insignia that meant he was a German.

He asked, "Do any of you have any experience in agriculture?" I was the only one who raised a hand. With a skeptical voice he asked, "What kind of experience do you have?"

I took my hat off, and in a straight, unafraid voice explained my experience with horses. After he finished asking his questions he showed us where our sleeping bunks were. They were the same as the first barrack I had been in. Each of us got one part of a three-tiered bunk. I always picked the upper deck for one reason; it was warmer.

By late afternoon, the rest of the inmates marched in. I saw them going directly to the pump, walking in twos. They washed and got ready for the Apel. Within half an hour, we heard the whistle and everyone was standing in line to be counted. The Kapo reported that everyone was there. Our hats were off and the counting began. The SS officer and recording soldier were counting, but when he came to our group of boys he stopped, and nodded his head like a greeting. I thought that I was mistaken, but it was confirmed later on that he had really done this.

When the Apel was finished, we all returned to the barrack and were surrounded by new inmates, who wanted to know when we had arrived and where we had come from. A short time later, food was brought in and every one was standing in line for our evening meal. To my surprise, we got our normal portion of soup, but there was also some vegetables and meat, and to finish it off, we got a nice slice of bread with a piece of margarine.

After everyone was finished, a short Jewish inmate came over carrying a violin and started to play. "We want to welcome you," he said. When he finished, another inmate started to sing, and this continued until the lights went out.

I noticed that the men were wearing different colored patches, and most inmates were not Jewish. I surmised that this was a political barrack and I wondered, "What kind of inmates were in the other barracks?" When I asked I was told, "Only Hungarians."

When the whistle blew the next morning, it was still dark. I jumped down from my bunk, ran outside to wash myself and then returned to the barrack. I made my bed, stood in line, got my slice of bread with margarine and got ready to go out for the Apel.

I noticed a man next to our bunk not eating his ration of bread, but was kneeling and praying. I approached him and asked him to get ready for the Apel. "Thank you son … don't worry, I will be ready."

As dawn appeared, the whistle blew, and we all stepped out for the Apel. I noticed that on the other side of the double wires there were other barracks. To my astonishment, I saw some women also assembling for an Apel. I guess I missed them the day before. They looked like little boys. Their hair was cut off and their uniforms were flat, like they didn't have breasts. I could not stop staring at them. They were being shaved by their Kapos. I also noticed that women in SS uniforms counted them. After the Apel, I was assigned to a group and marched to work with them. As I had hoped, I was going to work at a stable.

"You are the one who knows how to work with horses?" the inmate in charge asked.

"Yes sir."

"We have horses which some officer's ride." "How would you saddle this horse?" I felt good because I knew the answer.

"Sir, you would not saddle this horse, because this horse is a draft horse; they are a special breed of horse that are meant for heavy work."

"Well, you do know something about horses, but don't bluff too much, because what ever you don't know, I will teach you." I remained silent. I recognized that sometimes silence was golden.

I worked as hard as I could. I was cleaning the stable, brushing the horses and after they returned from the field, I made sure the horses drank enough water. "Hey Szlamek, (that was my name in Polish) come here!" the Kapo called. I felt a shiver going down my spine. I had witnessed how he whipped an inmate for no reason at all. What did I do wrong? I took my hat off and didn't say anything. "Come with me."

He took me to the corner of the last stall in the stable where there was a special horse, which belonged to an SS captain. He rode this horse three to four times a week. He loved this horse, but he didn't like people. This horse was as mean he was. "You have to take care of this horse. Every morning, you brush him, feed him and then take him to the water basin. Then dry him. Make sure he does not smell from the other horses. I will tell you when the officer wants to ride; you are going to saddle up the horse and wait outside for the officer to arrive. When he arrives, you take your hat off and hold the stirrups until he sits comfortably, and then hand the stirrup to him and move away quickly—or he purposely will run you over." That was some order! I was scared. I had a mean horse *and* a mean officer. What would be next?

Some time in September I heard the sweet voice of the Kapo summoning me like I was going to a firing squad. "Come here!"

I ran over to him and with my best voice said, "Yes Sir, what did I do wrong?"

"Did you finish with the morning chores?"

"Yes."

"You are going out to help a man plow the field with one of your horses. You will guide the horse and he will plow. The SS soldier will take you there. Take the wagon and pick up the plow and the inmate; he will take you both to the field. I was already tired. The Apel was at four thirty A.M.—why were they rushing us this morning. A thought went through my mind, "Are we really going to plow a field? What is the reason for plowing when they will never gain the fruit of our work?"

I felt tense. I didn't tell the other inmate, but I had made up my mind, that if the soldier went for his rifle, I was going to jump him. I was much stronger than when I had arrived. He was only one soldier.

My heart was beating—whatever was going to be was going to be—I was ready.

"Es ist ein schöner tag" [It is a nice day], the soldier said. I nodded back to him.

"Halt! Das ist der bereich" [Stop! That is the field]. I unhitched the horse. All the time I was standing on the other side of the horse, I was eyeing the soldier. We hooked up the plow and started working.

I introduced myself to the other inmate, "My name is Shloimo Vigdor but they call me Szlamek." He was a Hungarian Jew from Budapest.

"Halt! Das ist weit genug" [Stop! That is far enough]. Unhitch the horse from the plow and hitch it to the wagon. Now rest for awhile." We sat down on the wagon and looked toward the horizon; the sun was starting to set. We had been plowing for approximately six hours. We, and the horse, were dead tired.

# Yom Kippur 1944

I seemed as if I was in a trance, looking at the beautiful sunset, only to be awakened by the melody of Yom Kippur. The Hungarian chanted the prayer of Kol Nidre. After a while, we were ordered to drive back. Before we started, the Hungarian said, "You saw the field we plowed and you heard me chanting the Kol Nidre?"

"Yes."

"Well this is Erev Yom HaKippur. We turned over the soil which was covered with a grayish substance … those were the ashes from the crematorium. Maybe it was right for me to be here. Maybe those ashes were of my wife and my two small children, and as we were turning over the soil I buried them." At that point he quietly started to recite Kaddish with tears coming out of his eyes. He had arrived in Birkenau sometime in June, and went through the same regimen as I did. We both communicated in Yiddish.

As we were driving back, the SS soldier asked me what was wrong with the Hungarian. "Tonight is the beginning of the High Holy Day, and he misses being home." When we arrived back at the stable, we had just enough time for me to give water to the horse and bring him to his stall. As we were walking, the Kapo asked me whether we finished plowing the field. "No, we didn't, because the SS soldier told us to stop and we left the plow there."

"Then tomorrow you will have to go back."

"Sir, we just turned the soil over to cover up the ashes from the crematorium; can you get somebody else?" I asked with a pleading voice.

His face turned red with anger and he made sure that everyone heard him, "This is a concentration camp and you are going back!"

The next day I started my normal routine, but he didn't send me back to plow the field to cover up the ashes from the crematorium. For the next couple of days I could not shake off the terrible feeling that I walked on the ashes of thousands of Jewish remains. Sadness engulfed me, and once again I questioned my own existence. Why was I chosen to live, while so many were sent to the right to perish in the ovens? Even the Kapo noticed that since I had come back, I never smiled or pushed myself. About twenty inmates were working at the stable, most of them old timers. Working there, I was able to organize some food because they always brought in some vegetables for the horses. Normally on Sunday we worked a half-day, and the other part of the day we used to wash our own laundry.

The barrack had a choir and when they were done singing, some of the inmates entertained us. A violinist played and we had an opera vocalist who sang some arias. Those hours were quite entertaining, but like everything else it had to come to an end by lights out, and then we started our regimen all over the next day.

September was ending and we felt the chill in the air. It was Monday; we all knew what we had to do. I cleaned out the two stalls, put out some fresh straw, brushed and took the horses out to the trough to drink and then put in some fresh hay and barley for them to eat.

I was told that the SS captain was going to ride and I should get his horse ready. Immediately I saddled up his horse. It was a beautiful stallion, but he was hard to manage. There was a certain kind of meanness to this horse. I took him out to the trough to drink some water before the ride. Suddenly, he was trying to get away from me. Before I was able to contain him, he stood up on his hind legs. I was holding the horse's bridle with both hands and was not about to let go to be trampled. There I was, up in the air and still holding on to the bridle. The Kapo, the SS captain and several inmates were finally able to subdue the stallion. I was trembling not knowing what to expect next. I didn't know what precipitated the horse's behavior.

I heard the SS captain yelling at somebody who was screaming. I turned around, and it wasn't long before the screaming stopped. An inmate was lying in a puddle of blood. I witnessed the unmerciful beating to death of a person by horsewhip. Well, I was warned that we were nothing, whether we lived or died, it didn't make a difference. The captain turned away from the battered man, took his gloves off, threw them on the ground and looked at me. I thought that I was going to be blamed for something.

"What happened here," he said, "is that this man should have known better than to walk a mare in heat. But your horse taught you how to fly." I didn't see the humor.

# The Miracle

Some days later I developed a toothache and was brought to the veterinarian. She was a beautiful woman. When she touched me I started shivering. "I am not going to hurt you," she said with a smile. It wasn't the fear of hurting me; I was seventeen years old, and this was the closest I had ever been to a woman. She packed my tooth and told me to wait outside until it was time to go. I thanked her, while thinking I might just be having some more toothaches.

While waiting, I saw some pigs, and men walking with pails with hot potatoes. "This must be a good place to work," I thought to myself. Then I noticed the SS captain passing in front of me. Immediately I took off my hat, "Sir, my grandfather used to have a pig farm—I have some experience with pigs." He recognized me from the horse stable but didn't say anything and walked away.

That same evening, after the Apel, the Kapo assembled some of us and told us not to report to our regular work because we were going to work on the pig farm. I told some boys who were assigned what a bonanza had just been given to us. I also warned them about the captain, and told them about the incident with the horse and the inmate. "Remember what the Kapo in Birkenau told us. He said we don't have any value, so watch yourselves." By this time in my life I had learned a lot … mainly how to hate. But one thing my mind could not comprehend was how does anyone murder children?

It had been only six weeks since the doors of the train opened and I reminded myself that I had to live the way the man said. He was right; if I die, then nobody will remain from our family. They were not going to win this time. I was determined to survive. Deep within in me there was a rage to live, and no matter what, when it came to any decisions that I could make that might make survival a reality, I was going to make them.

The next morning, after the Apel, we were led to the pig stable. I was very nervous. What made me say that I had experience with pigs? The only thing I knew about pigs was when my uncle refused to let me play with my football, because the football was made out of pigskin. I was careful to observe what chores other people were doing with the pigs. We stood at attention and waited to be told what was expected of us.

"Achtung!" The sound vibrated through my bones.

Immediately our hats came off our heads as an elderly German Sergeant appeared. He stood for a while and looked at us. I was wondering what was going through his mind?

"You are going to cook potatoes for the pig feed. Watch yourselves; you are going to cook five to six hundred pounds of potatoes per day. You will cook the potatoes until this pool is full. You have to fill the potatoes in layers. After each layer of potatoes you will cover them with a layer of straw." At this point he turned us over to two Greeks from Salonica and we were divided into groups.

I had befriended two boys who must have come on the same transport as I did. I felt a certain kinship to them, and they felt the same about me. Their names were Yulek Zylbeger and Adek Wasercjer. Yulek and I were chosen to cook the potatoes. The next two had to wash the potatoes before we cooked them, and the rest were given choppers to chop them up. As the potatoes were brought to us, we put them in a twenty-four inch round, by five-foot high steamer until it was full. We closed the lid, opened the valves and let the steam do its job. We immediately walked away to the next steamer. When we finished with the last one, we returned to the first one. One Greek shut off the valves, released the door on the bottom and the first batch of potatoes rolled down to the wheelbarrow. The other Greek picked up the wheelbarrow and deposited the potatoes into the pond. Then we started the operation all over again. I was amazed at the speed at which we were cooking, and after we emptied the steamer, I kicked a couple potatoes off to the side for us to eat. The Greek didn't say anything. Whenever I bent down to pick up a potato, he and a wheelbarrow were blocking his view of me.

Yulek not only ate, but he tried to put some in his shirt for later. I warned him not to endanger himself. He chuckled about it, "Who is going to miss some potatoes here?" Slowly, over the next few days, the pond was filling up. Meanwhile, I kept observing how the people were working with the pigs. As I suspected, Yulek got caught filling his jacket with potatoes. He was taken into the shed and twenty lashes were meted out. Later on the same day, we were told that we were not needed any more and to report back to our previous work details. Well, it was nice while it lasted. As we were ready to depart, the Captain appeared. We were lined up and he was looking us over. Suddenly, he was pointing at me and wanted me to come forward. My heart was beating so strongly that I was afraid he might hear it. I took off my hat and stood up straight, facing him.

"You are coming back tomorrow. Report to me."

"Yavol, Herr Capitan." I turned around and went back to the line.

Because of the punishment Yulek could not sleep on his back for a while. I kept putting on wet rags to sooth his pain. All through this ordeal, he repeatedly said, "I know, I know ... don't say it ... you warned me."

The next day I reported with some other men to the pig stable. The first assignment was to round up marked pigs and load them on a wagon. With a loud scream, the pigs must have known that they were going to be slaughtered. I shuddered; the scream of the pigs was like the cry of little children. Is it possible that we are all reincarnations of different things? As the day progressed, the Kapo gave me the dirtiest jobs. I understood that I was new and I didn't care, as long I was able to organize some extra food.

Adek become my camp partner. Since I had food at the pig stable, I was able to share some with him. He and the rest of the boys didn't fare as well as I did. After they came back from work, and we had to stand for the Apel, they looked tired and worn. Sometimes we were standing for hours to be counted. Standing at attention, with the cold wind and rain thrashing us, the count finally began. The Kapos didn't care.

I was assigned to work in the stalls, where some of the sows were ready to furrow before having their young. I was told the normal litter was from six to eight at a time. My new occupation was to become a midwife for hogs. Besides delivering them, I was also taught to cut part of their fangs so that they would be forced to chew. I tattooed their ears with numbers for identification purposes. I must have been good at it because nobody was checking on me. I used to go and pick up some left over food from the SS mess hall, and also picked up milk to be mixed with the feeds for the young hogs. When I brought in the food nobody was watching me. I helped myself to the best food I could find, but I still had to be careful. Slowly my body started to fill in, and because I did a lot of physical work, I even started to develop some muscle.

One day I was sent out with a wagon to pick up potatoes and other vegetables. I was not guarded because it was within the confines of the camp. After picking up a full load, I turned around towards the pig stable. I stopped when some inmates with a wheelbarrow had to cross the road. There were about fifteen of them and they looked like skeletons.

Slowly I pulled the horse back and pretended that I had a problem. I walked over to the SS guard and asked if I could have a prisoner help me with the load. The SS guard didn't tell him, but with his rifle he chased him over to me. He was one of the Hungarians from the other block. I told him there was nothing wrong with my load, but that I was going to drop some potatoes and beets into the ditches where they were working. Everything worked out fine. Every time I shifted my weight, a couple of potatoes and beets rolled down the ditch. I nearly gave out more than I intended to.

I was not rushing myself to go back, because the Captain was out riding and I picked up a smaller load. It seemed my horse was getting tired. Everything would have been all right if the Captain would have still been out riding, but he was not.

"Where were you and why is the load so sparse?"

I told him what I had prepared in advance to say about the shifting load, but he didn't buy it. He took me into the shed, told me to bend over and with his whip in his hand said, "I want you to learn how to count. Starting now … count!" He started to whip me.

"One, two, three," I counted until I said "fifteen," and at that point he kicked me with his riding boot in my behind and I fell flat on my face. Well, I guessed that my profession as a pig farmer was over. I didn't understand. I ached, but it was not as painful as it could have been.

"How many did he give you?" my barrack mates wanted to know.

"Fifteen." To prove it, I removed my shirt.

"All we see are some red marks. He certainly didn't hit you too hard." I was surprised at hearing that. The next day I reported back to my station like nothing had happened.

The cold weather set in and certainly the winter snow would soon follow. We all shuddered when the first snow fell, knowing what to expect. Some of the boys came back from work. They could not open up their hands from working in the cold, frosty water trying to retrieve fish from the drained lake. Winter was never a friend to us. All it meant to us was a season to endure more pain. We heard that the crematorium and the gas chamber were blown up; what a pity it didn't happen before we arrived.

Pretty soon it would be Christmas. Even a Jew could celebrate the fact that, because it was Christmas, we would get some extra food. We all felt that the war was coming to an end, but how many more lives were going to be lost? On Christmas evening, some of the non-Jewish inmates were singing Christmas carols. We all felt the holiday spirit taking over the block. Sometime before the light was shut, a young SS Officer came in. We all jumped to our feet and stood at attention. He called us to get close together. "I came to wish you all a happy Christmas, and I hope that next year you all will be free; and I mean all of you! I want to shake your hands and also wish you a happy New Year." We were astounded to hear those words spoken by a German SS officer.

On New Year's morning, about fifty of our inmates were selected, including me, to go to the female camp. We didn't know what to expect, but we washed and wanted to look as presentable as possible. They escorted us to a hall and there were women as nervous as we were, waiting for us. A tall SS woman was standing in front of the female line.

"You are going to dance, but don't get too close," said the SS woman in a cordial voice.

At that point a man began to play the piano and slowly the men started to drift over to the female inmates. I was standing on the side because I didn't know how to dance, and I was too shy to hold a woman next to me. Every once in a while a man got a little too close to his female companion and the SS woman would tap the man on his head. I had tears in my eyes—what a horrible site this was—two zombies looking at each other with a far away look, remembering how things used to be.

When we all stopped dancing, we listened to some renderings from Mozart and Bach and finished with a song I will never forget: "*Mir Fahren zu America*" (We are going to America). I didn't know that this prediction would eventually apply to me. Fifteen days later, as the Russian's were approaching, we were marched toward Germany.

If anyone believes that my time in Auschwitz was a bed of roses they would be mistaken. There was not a moment that I forgot who I was and what it meant to those who had charge of my life. I was lucky to be in the right place at the right time. I was able to share some of my food with Adek Wasercier and others. The fear was always there, as well as the memory of losing, within one blink of my eyes, my mother and my siblings.

# Chapter 12

## A Ray of Hope

On the morning of January 15, we were told to get ready for evacuation. We were being moved to Buchenwald. For the past three months I had been working on the pig farm. The SS officer ordered us to slaughter all of the pigs before we left. This was a monumental undertaking because we were only fifteen workers and there were over one hundred pigs. The Germans didn't want to leave anything behind for the Russians. This was one of the hardest things I had ever done in the camps, because I had never slaughtered an animal before. By evening we were finished, and in our bloodstained clothes, we were ordered to march. We were rushed because we had to catch up with the others. As we marched, the temperature started to drop and it started to snow. Sometime during the night we caught up with our group who were sleeping in an abandoned wooden stall.

Our Kapo told us that we were going to sleep in the barn nearby. When we walked into the barn, it was filled to capacity. Our group, who had come late, had no place to lie down. We had to sleep wherever we could. We certainly could not sleep outdoors because we would have frozen to death. I looked around to find a place to lie down; I noticed a heavy beam above. That's where I slept for the remainder of the night.

At dawn we were reassembled, counted and ordered to march. I was tired from the night before and smelled from the pig blood, which started to get brown on my clothes. I caught up with Julek and Adek, and just having them near me gave me the strength to go on. Our clothing was not suited for the winter. We each had a single blanket; the only thing we had to protect ourselves from the extreme cold. We continuously heard the popping of gunshots. Every time we heard one, we knew that another human being just made it to heaven, because surely we were in hell. I don't remember if we had eaten anything that day.

# A Ray of Hope

Late on the third day, we came to a railroad station. I really do not know where that station was; it may have been Katowice. We were surrounded with SS soldiers and their dogs. They laughed as their dogs attempted to bite us. There were several groups of inmates from other camps. As we passed one of those groups, I heard my name being called. I turned around, and from a distance I saw my Uncle Moses waving at me. That little wave invigorated me; at least there was another person from our family alive. I waved back, and with tears in my eyes I yelled to him that I was doing fine. I hoped that I gave him what he had given to me. Then we were put in open iron/coal trains.

While we were traveling through many German cities, and passing under the bridges, the people were spitting down on us. They must have seen the dead bodies on one side, and on the other side a pitiful bunch of half-alive, near frozen, skeletal human beings. We were huddled together with blankets, which we had taken from the dead. By the time we arrived at Buchenwald, half of us had frozen to death. We were lucky that none of us had to go through a selection, because most of us would not have passed. In Buchenwald they didn't know what to do with us.

Buchenwald concentration camp was one of the largest in Germany, with 130 satellite camps and extension units. The name Buchenwald was given to the camp by Heinrich Himmler on July 28, 1937. The camp was established on July 16, 1937, when the first group of prisoners, consisting of 149 persons, mostly political detainees and criminals were brought to the site. Buchenwald was divided into three parts: the large camp, which housed prisoners with some seniority; the small camp, where prisoners were kept in quarantine and the tent camp, set up for Polish prisoners sent there after the invasion of Poland in 1939.

We were put in a barrack with 300 people. There were not enough sleeping bunks for everyone and some of us had to sleep on the ground. In the morning we got 200 grams of bread, a small piece of margarine and some ersatz coffee. In the evening we got a little watered down soup, with three small pieces of potatoes floating on top of it. We spent our twenty-four hours in the barracks with nothing to do. There were rows of barracks and between them were cattle wires, where we were permitted to walk around within the perimeter of our barrack. We could communicate with others, but we were not allowed to cross the wire barrier.

While I was walking around, I heard someone calling my name. I turned around and I saw Motek Lefkowicz, a childhood friend from Lódz. Both of us were overcome with emotion. We both thought that the other one was dead.

"Are you hungry Victor?" "If you are, I can give you some food every day."

He explained to me that he landed a job in a soup kitchen, and if I would look in a designated area at night I would find some bread and other things. At night I would sneak out and near the gate would find a parcel of food. This lasted for about a week. Then I heard that Motek was sent out from Buchenwald. I can truly say that he saved my life with that extra food. Through the years I thought about him and what he did for me. In 1995, when I met him in England at one of the reunions for "The Boys," I reminded him that he had helped me; but he didn't remember anything about it.

By the end of the month we were moved to Rehmsdorf. We arrived at around noon. The first thing we noticed were prisoners working with gloves on their hands. We also noticed the slime of oil all around us. It didn't take us too long to find out where the oil was coming from. We saw that oil drums had been blown up and the oil was still trickling from them. A little farther on we saw the devastation from the bombing that must have occurred a couple of days before.

We were assigned to a barrack and were given bunk beds to sleep in. It was just like Birkenau (Auschwitz); each bunk bed had five inmates and they were three rows high. However, unlike Auschwitz, the barracks were filthy. Around six o'clock we were called outside for the evening roll call. We waited for the other inmates to arrive. To our surprise, when they showed up, we noticed that what we thought were gloves on their hands was dirt mixed with oil sludge. Rehmsdorf was a huge chemical industrial complex. They were able to extract gas from coal at this facility. At the time I didn't know other chemicals were also manufactured there.

Within a couple of days, we were as dirty as the other inmates. The water was rationed, and with the little water we were able to obtain, we had to wash our laundry and ourselves. In Auschwitz we had to wash up when we came back from work, and if one was caught dirty, the whole block suffered the consequences. We had two sets of uniforms and we wore one while the other was being washed and hung up to dry. In the morning we washed up, and then went for the Apel to be counted.

Rehmsdorf was not the same. We went to sleep dirty and woke up dirty. The bed bugs and the lice had a feast with our bodies. The food ration was the same as it was in Buchenwald, but this time we had to labor for it. We were working in the midst of German civilian workers. They saw our wretched bodies and sunken eyes, which were begging for some food, but none of them volunteered to give us any. There were frequent bombings. We were not concerned about the bombings. We didn't mind the bombings. We knew the war was winding down, soon to be over, and the bombings were in our favor. When we heard the sirens we knew that the area we were going to would be hit, but we didn't care. Gazing up at the sky, we saw wave after wave of planes coming in our direction. We were put in a gorge where we were kept until the bombing was over. How beautiful those planes were. They were like eagles, high in the sky with white vapor trailing.

We had heard that if you worked certain jobs you were given some soup for lunch. It didn't take too long before Julek and I secured jobs. What I didn't know was that I was going to become an expert in digging out unexploded bombs. It was dangerous, but that extra soup was a lifesaver. Sometimes those bombs were as much as eight feet down.

First, we had to dig around the bombs and the tip was always at the deepest end. It had rained for the past couple of weeks, and most of the time the lower part was immersed in water. Maybe Julek and I were lucky, since neither of us was killed. Sometimes the bomb broke in half and the yellow explosive powder got wet. That kept the bomb from blowing up in our faces.

When it got dark we dragged ourselves back to the barracks half-alive. After the Apel we got our liter of soup. You would think that we would rest, but we started to talk about how we outwitted the Germans. Some of us were even able to organize some extra food. Due to the constant rain, and to our dismay, the Allies had not recently bombed our complex.

Once again, my unexpected luck played a role that saved Julek's and my life. As I was standing in line to go to work, I was pushed back three lines behind Julek. Those of us in the rear were assigned to clean bricks from bombed out buildings. While we were working, I started to whistle when I noticed an SS officer observing me and smiling. He looked different. His hair was gray and his face was not as stern as the others. He motioned to me to follow him. He stopped and asked if I spoke German. Without any hesitation I said, "Jawohl." He took me to a hut and told me to take care of it. I looked around and noticed SS soldiers at a long table sitting around and reading newspapers. At the same time my eye also spotted a shelf above the table lined with canteens. I immediately knew I hit the jackpot! This was the SS mess hall, and there was another room around the corner where the French prisoners of war were having their meals. They were housed in the next hut. Whenever they received packages of food from the Red Cross, they shared some with me and in turn, I shared with Julek. Adek had a position with a Kapo, and was also able to obtain some food. The officer showed me his office and told me what he expected of me. I was left alone and was very uneasy with the SS around me. What a dump that hut was! Immediately, I knew what I had to do. I needed a lot of soap, water and some paint to brighten up the place.

The next day I found out that the officer was a Major. He could have been in his sixties, and if so, might have obtained his rank during the First World War. I started to work on his office first. It didn't take long before I had his office spotless. I asked certain SS soldiers not to wash their canteens in cold water. I told them that I would clean them. When I was finished with the canteens, they looked like new. Within two weeks I had approximately twenty canteens, and most of them had some food left in them. As time passed, I became at ease with everyone. But not for one minute did I forget my place and who I was. I knew I had to play their game. I never wore my hat inside the hut; therefore I didn't have to take it off for them. I kept myself spotless. I shaved off every hair on my body and organized another set of uniforms, which I kept in the hut.

Working there I got to know many German SS. At times there were some high-ranking officers sitting around the table discussing their war stories. Normally, I brought some ersatz coffee or schnapps, and they just chattered away like I didn't exist. I tried to stay out of harm's way. Many times the Major engaged me in conversations regarding my being there. He asked me, "Where were you born?" "How much schooling do you have?" "Where did you learn to speak the German language?"

Most of the time I told him what he wanted to hear. During one of these chats at the table, an officer asked me in a half-drunk tone, "Hei Victor, wo ist deine familie" [Where is your family]? I was not a hero, my heart was in my throat ... but I blurted out about the ghetto, Auschwitz and how I found out what happened to my mother, brother and sister. I also told them about the children who perished in the gas chambers. This was my way for them to hear the truth, so that none of them, in the future, would be able to deny that they didn't know. I might never have another opportunity to face a German again and speak with such boldness. I must have spoken for about half an hour, when the drunken officer quietly said, "Das ist genug" [That is enough]. There was an eerie silence. I was seventeen-years old, and holding back my feelings. I was not about to show them the tears in my eyes. I walked out of the hut, and all of the memories, pain and guilt from Auschwitz resurfaced. It still hurts. Today, I wonder how I had the guts and dared to stand up and face them. Personally, I think I must have been temporarily insane.

There were other things I had done while I was there and if I had gotten caught, the consequences would not have affected anyone but me. I didn't have to worry about my family. Even today, in my mind, I can see my little sister and the rest of the family. That picture never leaves me. When I was young I was told I was born with a gold spoon in my hand. Is that why I am here today? I cannot explain a lot of things, including working at the SS hut.

The Major lived in a nearby city and used to go home for the weekends. When he would come back, he would ask me how I felt. Not only that, he brought back some home cooked food. It wasn't much, but it sustained me for another day. After a few weekends, something about the Major changed. Was it the realization that Germany was losing the war? Or had he heard about Auschwitz for the first time?

A week before we had to be evacuated from Rehmsdorf, the Major asked me whether I would visit him after the war. I never thought a German would ever put a question like that to me, nor did I want to answer. Yes, he was trying to be nice, but he was wearing an SS uniform, with plenty of medals. As I looked at him I thought, "If our roads ever cross again, and I have the means, I most probably will kill you." But, if given the opportunity, could I have done it? I don't know. A couple of days later we were all evacuated from Rehmsdorf, and I never saw the Major again.

In mid-April, as the Allies were approaching Rehmsdorf, we were put on open cattle trains and evacuated. They selected eighty prisoners for each train. Because it was April, not January like the last time we were moved, we were a little better prepared. We took our blankets and one day's provisions. Most of the prisoners were young like myself. Under these conditions we had a better chance of survival. One of the Germans who knew me, ordered me to create a corner where he would sleep and guard us. Julek, Adek and I did what I was told, and it was also our place to sleep. While everybody was packed in, we at least were able to sleep comfortably.

The train was moving south. It was weaving through the mountains and climbing higher and higher. At the railroad station, the train finally stopped. The sign said, "Welcome to Marienbad." It was Czechoslovakia. The air was pure and cold. This was the Spa that was famous throughout Europe. The whistle blew; all of the SS stepped off and lined themselves around the train. None of us knew what would happen next. We were watching for their next move. We were not afraid … I don't know why. Was it because we were young? Was it because we knew the Allies were all around us?

The SS were fed, and then we were told to disembark from our trains. Under the watchful observation of our guards, we were given our first and only meal for the day. For the next couple of days we were allowed to walk around the trains and mingle with each other. What helped us was that I knew some of the Germans. This gave me the opportunity to organize some food. Even in the middle of April the nights were horrendous. Most of the guys were starving. The cold and the frost were unbearable. We hoped that we would be liberated here and now! The Allies surrounded us, but we didn't know which Allies. We knew that it was only a matter of days or hours and we would be free. Therefore, we were cautious not to do anything foolish.

Every once in a while I would engage in a conversation with a young, redheaded Ukrainian SS guard.[18] He was one of the guards who reported to the Major, whom I worked for in Rehmsdorf. He was also assigned to guard a certain section where camp inmates were working. He looked about two years older than I was and had some college education. Now he was guarding our supply train. Once he asked me whether I missed the Major. Of course I said that I did, but I didn't mean it.

Around the third day at Marienbad, I was about to walk toward him, and noticed that he was watching somebody under the supply train. It was a young Hungarian boy whom I had befriended in Auschwitz, who always smiled and greeted me. Whenever I was able to help him, I did. He also lost his family in Bierkanau. All of us tried to protect our younger boys whenever we could, especially when there were selections to work. They were always put in the back so that they could stand on their toes to make them look a little bit taller.

I noticed that he was under our supply train and trying to scoop up something into his hat. Whatever it was, it was trickling down onto the railroad tracks. It looked like sugar. I noticed that the Ukrainian was also eyeing him. What was he doing under there? He should have known better.

The Ukrainian removed his rifle from his back … my heart stopped. I was walking toward the SS guard hoping that he would start to talk to me and forget about the kid, but he ordered me to go back. I wanted to call to him to run away, but it was too late. The SS guard called the boy over, and looked into his hat. He must have seen what he had in it. I heard the kid pleading with him, but to no avail. I already knew what the outcome was going to be. The guard led him into the forest—I heard a shot.

---

[18] Germans were not the only component of the SS. *Jewish Virtual Library*, accessed 9/23/2010, http://www.jewishvirtuallibrary.org/ jsource/Holocaust/ waffenss.html.

In my short life I saw thousands of people die, so what was so special about him? Was it that he was the same age as my brother would have been? In his hat, he had a spoonful of sugar. Did he have to die for that? Didn't God know that he was the last of his family? For six years he fought to survive, only to die three weeks before the end of the war. What is life all about? He was only fourteen-years old. Where was the Almighty to permit things like this to happen? The haunting memory of this young boy has always lingered in my mind. At Yom HaShoah, the yearly Holocaust Remembrance Day, I always light a candle for him and for the other victims of the Holocaust. I also made a promise, that if I ever wrote about my life, I would mention this young boy. He wanted to live, but his life was shortened on top of the beautiful mountain called Marienbad. I don't remember his name any more, but I know it is my duty to remember him, because if I don't, it would be like he never even existed.

# Chapter 13

## Escape, Capture and A Birthday Present

*Mirror*

We thought for sure that we were going to be liberated. The Allies were all around us, but at the last minute the Germans were able to get us back onto the trains. It seems they had found another escape route. As the train was descending the mountain, we noticed that planes were coming directly toward us. Before we could respond, the train engine was bombed and we were strafed from all sides with machine guns.

The Allied planes mistook us for a German army movement. I don't remember how I cleared or jumped from the train. All I remember is trying to dodge bullets.

Julek, Adek and I realized we were in the forest. I read in the newspaper many years later that we lost over six hundred people at that time. We were free and we were escaping into the forest with the hope that we might encounter some Allied soldiers. Our faces were torn from the branches of the young trees, but we didn't feel any pain. We were free, we were exhilarated, we jumped through streams and we were bubbling with excitement. "Did you ... did you see?" we kept repeating over and over again.

We ran for about five or six hours and were exhausted. We came upon a valley, and from the distance we saw that there were three houses. We needed help to get out of the forest, and we were also hungry. Julek decided to go down and fetch some food and clothes. We watched Julek as he walked down into the valley and entered the first house. He disappeared behind the door. It took quite a while until we became annoyed with him and jokingly I said, "Julek must be having a nice meal down there."

We were ready to join him when we noticed that the door opened and Julek came out with his hands up. Nobody had to explain to us what it meant ... he got caught. We were ready to run away because there was nothing we could have done for him. We felt we must save our own lives. We turned around and saw two Hitler Youth aiming their submachine guns at us. We raised our hands above our heads. We knew what it meant; we most probably were going to be shot—unless we did something. This was just like the ghetto when I had been caught and escaped. I knew that I would have to do something, but I could not convey my thought to Julek or Adek.

Meanwhile, we were turned over to an older soldier carrying a rifle that must have been from the French Revolution. There was the possibility that one of us was going to be killed. We saw a village in the distance, and Julek decided to engage the German in conversation. With a pleading voice, Julek begged the German to let us go. We explained that if any harm came to us, he would be held responsible. He motioned for us to sit down, took out a piece of bread and cheese from his knapsack and told us to share it with each other. We sat down and it didn't take us long to finish it off. We looked at the soldier. He appeared to be in his sixties, but then again, the stress of war can make any man look older. We decided once again to plead for our lives. All he was able to tell us was that he was ordered to deliver us to the local SS command. We concluded that if he delivered us to the authorities, we probably would be shot.

As we were trudging along, I noticed that a German officer was approaching us. He offered a cigarette to the old soldier, and then they were talking for a while. We didn't hear what was said, but I recognized that he was the officer who asked me what happened to my family. For a while I thought that he would take pleasure in finishing the job himself. He turned towards me and asked what I was doing here. He looked tired and rundown. I explained to him that when the planes strafed us, we jumped from the train and ran into the nearest forest to save our lives, and got lost. The officer turned around to the soldier and explained that he would turn us in to the proper authorities.

We stopped at the nearest stream, washed ourselves and rested for a while. When we started to walk again, I asked him if he wanted me to carry his pack. He seemed to trust me and nodded yes. As we were walking in front of him, I decided to engage him in conversation. Very cautiously I asked him whether he realized that he was now in Czechoslovakia. I also told him that if we walked and talked with him, we might protect him from the partisans. He looked frightened and kept looking around. I thanked him for saving our lives. I was sure that I gave him something to think about. He was in as much danger from the partisans as we were, if he turned us into the authorities.

At that point, Adek and Julek closed ranks with me and we all started to talk. The officer even smiled, but we really didn't know what was on his mind. Somehow he knew where to walk, because a little later we caught up with what was left of our train transport. He spoke to another officer, and then came over to us and told us that he would pick us up in the morning. I didn't know what was on his mind. If he was going to kill us he had every chance to do so. The only thing I could think of was that he was as frightened as we were. The next morning, at dawn, he was already standing near the gate waiting for us.

I don't remember how many days we walked, but as long as we were with this officer we were able to acquire some extra food. I don't even remember whether Julek and Adek were walking with me every day. What I do remember is that during the last two days of our march, the officer disappeared and we never saw him again. It seems that a day before we arrived at Leitmeritz, a couple of kilometers before Theresienstadt, we went through a small village, but I don't recall its name.

At that time we must have looked awful. Many of us didn't have shoes, and some of us had to help others to walk. Some were beyond help because they were no more than walking skeletons. We didn't want to lose any more people. We all sensed that we were really going to reach our destination. Life was becoming so very precious. Once again, I acknowledged that rage to live, so deep within me. To survive all this meant to have a life, and it meant that Hitler would not win. We tried to muster courage with all the sense of hope we had left in us.

Every Passover, we read in the Haggadah how God supplied manna for the Israelites in the desert. Well, another miracle happened in this little village. From the opened windows, loaves of bread were flying out towards us. We scrambled for them. Julek caught one, immediately hid it in his jacket and laid down on the ground like he was sick, until we came to him. Julek shared the bread with us, and we survived another day.

One week later we arrived in the Theresienstadt Ghetto. I cannot honestly say how long or what distance we walked; whether it was a week or six days. All I know is that we marched, and after each day was over, whenever and wherever an officer told us to sleep, we did. We were thankful that another day had passed and we were still alive. We all believed that liberation might be within hours. But how many other times did we have that same hope? When we walked into Theresienstadt, the sight of women and children was too much. We thought that we would never see another Jewish child alive. Most of us were hardened by our circumstances, and we believed that nothing could affect us anymore. But, seeing children once again was emotionally overwhelming.

Some people came to welcome us. We were not in a mood to be welcomed. The night before we had slept outdoors and we were tired and hungry. They divided us, and we were led to the top of one of the fortification walls before we were assigned to our buildings. These walls were very wide. Theresienstadt was originally built as a fortified town, surrounded by two sets of brick walls, with bastions jutting out on all sides, resembling the points of a star. There was a wide moat between the walls. There were ramparts and barracks for soldiers with a fortress like this, and the ramparts were very wide. It was large, like a medieval castle. Many people could walk on those ramparts.

Women came with some bread, which they tried to distribute. I don't know what they were thinking. Did they think that we were normal, or civilized, or that we were going to stay orderly and in line? People hadn't eaten for the last two days. Some of the guys jumped onto the women to get the bread; those well meaning ladies barely escaped with their lives. Julek jumped into the center, and the only thing I saw of him were his legs. It might seem funny now, but then it was a matter of sheer survival. We didn't need that piece of bread at that moment, but what about tomorrow? Adek and I jumped in and pulled Julek out by his legs while he was still clutching a piece of bread. While we were pulling Julek, two people were fighting for a piece of bread. They both stumbled and fell from the rampart and got killed. This was eight days before the end of the war and their liberation. Julek shared the piece of bread with us. We survived another day and we were thankful. Before the day was over, we were put in a building, the Hamburger Kasserne, with twenty-five other people. I slept with one flimsy blanket, with my clothes on—the thin pants issued to me in Auschwitz, the stripped jacket with my yellow and red Star of David and my number—B7568.

## The Russians Are Coming

Ten days after our arrival in Theresienstadt, at 10 A.M., I heard a commotion, "The Russians are here." I started walking out of my room, which I shared with thirty others. Planes had been bombing the area every day for eight or nine hours. You could hear them and see the smoke from the targets that were being hit. We knew it was just a matter of time and the war would end … would it be tomorrow?

I was ill. I had a slight case of dysentery and I had just come out of the bathroom. When I heard the news, I felt a little dizzy. I was holding on to the door handle and trying to formulate in my own mind what I had just heard; I closed my eyes.

People were running down the hall, someone brushed against me and I almost fell down. I heard hundreds of voices crying. I knew what was happening … the war was over. I didn't jump for joy. I thought, "I am alive. I won. No matter what I have lost, I won. I am alive." I had waited six years for this moment … freedom. I said to myself, "What does it mean? Am I a human being again? Does it mean I can go to sleep and not be afraid? Does it mean that I just might have enough to eat and not go to sleep hungry? Six years of slavery and now I am free … free for what?" When we arrived at Birkenau, I stood frozen in fear and confusion, and now, for a moment, the same thing occurred. I remembered what the man told me in Auschwitz, "If you die, then Hitler will succeed. Therefore, you have no choice but to live." I won and I survived, but it seemed such a hollow victory.

We broke down the gates of the camp; there were no Germans to stop us because they had all run into the woods. We saw the Russian tanks advancing toward the camp and we ran to meet them. I saw soldiers on a tank, I tried to run up to them, but I was not strong enough to continue. A tank stopped, and one of the soldiers stretched out his hand and lifted me up onto the top of the tank. I grabbed him, gave him a hug and kissed him. It's hard to describe the feeling of that moment. It's like all your life you wanted this beautiful, expensive toy and all of a sudden it's in your hands, it's all yours, but you don't know what to do with it. The emotion was paralyzing. With tears in my eyes and in his, he whispered very quietly, "A Yid?" He must have noticed the yellow and red star with my number on my uniform.

The soldier's face was dirty, not shaven, his eyes were bloodshot and he also smelled; he probably had not changed his clothes for some time. While I was riding on the tank he gave me some dark bread with butter, and once again very quietly said, "Shalom." The tank stopped and I got off wondering why he had whispered the first and second greeting. Was it anti-Semitism? Mulling over my thought, I wobbled back to Theresienstadt.

Once the Russians got to our camp, they started rounding up the Germans that had fled. They offered us machine guns and we were told, "You are entitled to kill a few Germans if you want to after what they did to you." A Russian put a machine gun in my hands. I played with it, like a toy, firing it a few times at nothing in particular. I went into the woods to hunt for Nazis and I saw a young airman. He looked to be about my age. He started to come out of the forest, walking toward me. I had the gun—I had the power—for once the Nazi was the little man and I was the big man! I told him to lift his arms and to loosen his belt. I was alone in the woods with this Nazi and a gun, the trigger was cocked and I wanted to kill him. I kept wishing that he would try to shoot at me to give me an excuse to fire back, but he looked too afraid to make a move. I couldn't do it. I had seen enough death. The war was over and I just wanted to get on with my life. I don't think any of the camp survivors killed a German that day. We may have been more inclined to shoot if we found any SS, but they were long gone.

A number of us started to hunt for something more important, something we really wanted—food. I went to the next town and raided a warehouse. I ate the first thing I grabbed—a 3 1/2 pound can of lard. I ate every bit of it and it tasted so good. This was real freedom after years of starving. I returned to the barracks with chickens, potatoes and fish. We burned chairs to keep the fire going so we could cook. I don't remember anyone talking, just eating. Then we would sleep, wake up and eat some more. I moved over to a corner in the room and remembered the last time I saw my mother, brother and sister at Bierkenau. I was free and I began crying like a baby and pulled my blanket around me. I was still cold, so I hugged my knees and thought, "How thin you are Victor." I had no hair and I weighed 110 pounds. I had no education, no family, no money, no trade—no idea of what to do next. I was not weak, but neither was I strong, yet I was in much better physical condition than many of the others. The first thing I was going to do was get well. Then I was going to go back to Lódz to see if someone from my family, or anyone I knew, had survived. But first I decided to go and talk to the Russians. All I could think was, "You have to start over, like a baby that has just been born. You have to grow up and learn to be a man." This was my last thought on May 8, 1945—the day of my liberation, and my eighteenth birthday.

# Chapter 14

## I Will Surpass You

The Russians gathered all the youngsters to a central place with better quarters and better food. Within four weeks we started to physically improve. It didn't take long before food started to flow into Theresienstadt, and so did some of the other things that are present by the end of most wars: typhus fever, dysentery and tuberculosis. Once again, death made its entrance into our lives.

"How old are you?"

I was asked this question by an investigator from the British Jewish Joint Committee. They came to Theresienstadt to look for young camp survivors. They were authorized to bring 1,000 to England. The age of refugees was limited to sixteen years old. I was briefed by an official before my interview and told to lie about my age. I was exactly eighteen years old. My hair was cut off for health reasons, and at only 110 pounds I could easily pass for a fourteen year old. When interviewed I knew what to say, "Sir, I am fourteen years old."

Julek and Adek also signed up to go to England. We were subjected to a medical exam and approved for transport, which would occur at the end of July. However, the Russians wanted us to go to Russia. The Russian commander of Theresienstadt had a very sweet carrot for us. He promised us a free education at the University of Moscow.

While we were waiting for transport day, some of us went back to our home countries to look for our families and other survivors. Julek Zylberger, my partner in the concentration camps, had contracted typhus and couldn't travel. I had a touch of dysentery from eating food that I was not accustomed to. One day I found two cans of lard and ate all of it. I paid the price for that! Adek Wasercijer left for Lódz, and I was stuck in Theresienstadt. I also wanted to go back to Lódz; maybe I would find someone I knew who was alive. In my mind I knew that nobody had survived, but there was still a glimmer of hope.

# I Will Surpass You

I went to see the Russian doctor and asked him about Julek's condition. The prognosis was not good. His fever had not subsided. I decided not to leave him until he got healthier; then I would go to Lódz. Two of my friends had already died from typhus, and I was scared for Julek. I thought of him as my own brother. We suffered together through many camps, and now, after six years of fighting for our lives and being liberated, he might now die. However, the good news did come a few days later; his fever dropped, but it would take four weeks before he could be released. I was not permitted to see him. I wrote him a note and let him know that I was going to Lódz and I would wait for him there.

On the journey to Lódz, I arrived in Krakow around noon. The station was full of returnees, most of whom were not Jewish. All of them were interested in their train schedules. I saw a man who was still wearing the stripes from the concentration camp. I tried to approach him, and two Polish people started to question him, "Hey Jew, where are you going? Why aren't you going to Palestine? We don't want you here!" I was dumbfounded. I saw tears come down the man's face, and nobody came to his defense. I was scared too, and angry. How dare they? Yes, I am a Jew, but I am also a Pole. How dare they? I noticed a multitude of people looking at me. I met their glare of hate with my own hate.

I felt like shouting at them, "You didn't help us; you turned us in —you are worse than the Germans. I watched you in the ghetto through the barbed wire and saw how your stores were full of meats, fruits, dairies and other commodities, while we were starving. You could have helped us but you didn't. My father fought for Polish independence in WW I and was wounded. He received a medal for valor. He died in the ghetto at the age of forty-one, in poor health compounded by the wound he got defending the border at Romania. He returned to be with his family, only to die in the ghetto. He loved Poland, and so did I. I don't need you! I have a choice. I am going back to Theresienstadt. From there I will go to Palestine or to England. I swear I will never come back to Poland. I will forget you … and your anti-Semitism … and your language … and forget you ever existed! I am a survivor. I will get married and build a new family, and let me assure you … I will surpass you!"

I immediately went back to Theresienstadt. Two weeks later, Adec came back from Lódz. I closed the gate of no return to Poland forever ... or so I thought.

By the end of July we were told to get ready to leave.

# Chapter 15

## The White Cliffs of Dover

Hamburger Kassern was the place where we were housed until we left for Prague. The night before we were to leave, at about 10 P.M., the Russian commander came in unexpectedly. He didn't need to introduce himself because he had been very helpful to all of us. Many times, when somebody needed food or medicine, we knew whom to turn to, but this time he looked stern. He had two soldiers with him. As he looked us over I felt a shiver down my back. I wondered if he was a Russian German.

He tried, for the last time, to persuade us to go to Russia. When he realized he was not succeeding, he commented, "You suffered, we suffered, we also liberated you; within five years you are going to come back and fight us." We were appalled.

"We will never fight you. You liberated us and we will never forget it." We were just tired of commissars. England promised us the same package and more—at a future date we thought we would be transferred to Palestine. We all experienced some guilt. The Russians fought and died while liberating us. They treated us well and took care of our sick.

Finally he spoke, "Every one, stand up. I want to be serious. We want all of you to come to Russia to attend Moscow University to start a new life. I will give you twenty-four hours to think it over. We liberated you and brought you back to health. If you go to England, and most likely there is going to be another war, you are going to be involved in it against us."

Our faces turned white and we started to protest, "We will never fight the Russians. You were very helpful and most of us know how much we have to thank the Russian soldiers."

He began walking toward the door. Without turning around he said, "You have twenty-four hours."

Two days later the British Jewish Commission returned to Therezeinstadt to inspect us. Within one week we were supposed to be going by train to Prague and from there by plane to England. Three of our boys did go to Russia. We all felt badly about leaving the Russian soldiers. We got our passports from the Russians, with the stipulation that we would go to England as students and that our final destination would be Palestine. The next day we left for Prague.

In the morning there were two lorries waiting for us. Everyone was ready except me. I told our leader that I would not go without Yulek Zylberger. With luck, three of us were able to bring him out of the hospital to one of the lorries. He looked like a chicken without any hair, but he was alive. I could not leave without him. Everyone was cheering as the lorries started to move toward Prague. When we arrived in Prague, we were told that there was a storm brewing in the Atlantic, and the planes would be delayed until it would be safe to fly. The rain appeared on the horizon as predicted. We were placed in two hotels and both were in the center of the old town.

"Children," our supervisor said, "you are in the center of Jewish life in Prague as it used to be. If you go out from the hotel, make a right turn until you come to the Josefov area and keep going until the end. Then you will arrive at the Old New Synagogue." I asked Yulek to join me, but he thought that I was crazy to go out in the bad weather. He reminded me that I was free to explore Prague, but that I had to report to him when I came back. Most of the boys decided to rest up after the long journey from Therezinstadt.

It didn't take me long to find Josefov. This is the area where most of the Jews had lived. I walked past an old synagogue, and there was a cemetery with memorial stones that were quite dilapidated and lying all over the ground. I came to what looked like a temple. It was falling to pieces. On the top it had a clock with the Hebrew alphabet. I went inside and a woman greeted me, "Welcome to the Old New Synagogue. My name is Hannah. There is a fee of ten corons." I didn't have any money.

"I just came from Therezinstadt." The woman looked at me like I had just come back from the dead. She was silent and tears appeared in her eyes. I didn't know what to do or say.

After a while she composed herself and said, "I lost my whole family there. How did you make out?"

"I lost my family in Kaminsk, the Lódz ghetto and Bierkenau." Once again there was silence.

"You don't have to pay. You already paid and I will be your guide. You are going to have lunch with me." She sounded like a commandant in camp. I started to laugh and so did she.

She must have been a good-looking woman when she was young, but now there was so much pain in her face. She wiped her face and once again a smile appeared as she started to speak about the synagogue, which dated back to the middle of the thirteenth century. It was the oldest synagogue in central Europe. There are many legends about this building. One of the claims is that angels came with Jerusalem stones when the synagogue was being built, and they had protected the temple ever since. I was mesmerized by what I was seeing and couldn't believe that the Nazis left Prague without destroying this magnificent temple. I was reading and looking at all the articles, artifacts and pictures. Those were not just pictures—they were Holocaust survivors. To me they were messages of people, Jewish people talking from the past. I didn't notice how much time had passed. She reminded me that we had a lunch date. I noticed stairs going up to another floor with a chain across it.

"What are the secrets hidden above the stairs?" I meant it as a joke, but I looked at her face for an answer?

"There are no secrets above those stairs, it is just our heritage. If you want to go up you may."

"What is the mystery?"

"There is no mystery … women are not allowed to enter that room."

Slowly I started to walk up the stairs; my heart was beating. What was in this room that did not allow women to go in? When I entered (there is no public access to the attic anymore), there was a small window. It gave just enough light to see a white stucco object, covered like a coffin. There was a sign above it, which read, "Here sleeps the Golem for eternity, and shall be awakened when in need." I remembered my mother's version (there are many versions) of the story about the creation of the Golem, by Rabbi Loew of Prague.

It was sometime in 1500, when the Jews of Prague were oppressed by their Catholic neighbors. There was a new danger brewing in Prague. A priest planned to accuse Jews of a new ritual murder. When Rabbi Loew heard this, he prayed to heaven to help him save his people. He searched the Kabbala for knowledge and found the way to make a Golem. He had to take clay from the riverbed, sculpt the likeness of a human being and let it dry until the clay was red. He brought two students to help. They molded the clay. It had to be seven feet tall. Then Rabbi Loew and a student walked seven times around it, chanting prayers to the Almighty for help. When the prayers were finished, Rabbi Loew picked a piece of holy parchment and put it on the Golem's lips. Again Rabbi Loew walked around seven times, bent over the figure, blew air in the Golem's nostrils and the Golem opened his eyes. "Stand up and defend us from all who want to hurt our people!" The Golem stood up and went to the gate and defended the ghetto against all who wanted to do harm to Rabbi Loew's people. When the task was finished, Rabbi Loew commanded the Golem to return to the temple and lay down to sleep. The Golem closed his eyes. The Rabbi prayed to the Almighty, "Wake him up when Jews are in danger."

There I was, standing in front of what was supposed to be the sleeping Golem's entombment, thinking that if he had awakened how many children could have been saved? Oh Rabbi Loew, why did you put him to sleep? I wondered if my mother had just told me a tale, or if the Golem really existed? I slowly walked down the stairs.

Hannah was waiting for me. "Are you ready for lunch?" Without a word spoken I walked over to her and squeezed her hand. She smiled at me and I smiled too.

During the next four days I went through the National museum, and for the first time in my life saw an opera with Julek. I also visited the Palace where President Edward Benes lived. I went to the old market, which had a clock that was at least two hundred years old. Of course, every day I saw at least two movies. Just four months earlier I was wearing concentration camp striped garb with a number, B7568. But now I was called by my own name, because Victor Breitburg really existed again.

After four days, the deluge subsided and we welcomed the sun. We arrived at the airport, and there were ten, four engine Lancaster bombers from the British Air Force on the runway. They were the shining eagles in the blue sky with the white vapor trails. The last time I saw them was when they were flying over Rehmsdorf, bombing the oil installation where I was working. How we had cheered them— never giving a thought that we might also get killed.

The excitement started to build up in all of us. Some of us shared one last thought about the Russians ... we were really leaving them. I was never near a plane at any time in my life, and now I was going to England in one. I touched the plane as if it were a precious gem in a child's hands.

In the midst of all the excitement, I never gave a thought that we were going to a country with a foreign language. I knew that I was leaving the horrors of the war behind me. I knew that I was going to a country that had so gallantly fought and sacrificed their own lives to defeat the Nazi hordes. Certain practical realities were not yet being considered.

An English pilot spoke to us in German and asked us to board the planes. As we started walking up the stairs to the airplane door, we noticed that there was a crowd of people who came to see us off. There was a commotion. I turned around to see what was happening—one of our girls was screaming and running down toward the crowd of people. For a minute we all were stunned. In that crowd, this girl found her mother and sister whom she believed were dead. There was not a dry eye among the crowd or us. Ten minutes later we would have been up in the air flying, and these three people would have missed each other. I don't remember whether the girl went with us or remained in Prague. As the plane taxied down the runway, we descended into complete silence. We were finally leaving the part of Europe that we were familiar with, and going to a new world.

Three hundred boys and fifteen girls, young Holocaust survivors, left Theresienstadt for England to face a better tomorrow. Questions were common among us: "Will we have to learn a strange language?" "What do they expect from us?" "Are they expecting only sixteen year old and younger children?"

I had many questions of my own. I was not as confident as Julek. I admired him for that. He was one year younger than I was. When we were in Prague, it was he who insisted that we go to the opera. What did I know about opera? He was far more advanced in these areas than

I was, but I eventually caught up. My thoughts were about my future. We were free now, but to whom were we going to turn for help? None of us had any family. I knew about my two aunts in America, but I didn't know their full names, or which part of New York they were residing in. I decided to try to work it out once I was in England.

A little time elapsed and we were over Germany. I looked out from the small window in the plane, and I noticed the devastation of the town we had just passed by. The walls were still standing, but everything else was gutted. The streets were obliterated with ruins from falling bricks that once were buildings. I didn't feel sorry for the people below. They brought it upon themselves. But until I saw it, I never realized how great the devastation was. I guess they have to thank Adolf Hitler for that. This was the Third Reich, which was supposed to have lasted a thousand years. How many innocent children, on both sides, died?

"Well, Herr Hitler," I thought, "you didn't succeed. If you had succeeded with us, would you have closed the concentration camps? Would everyone have lived in a Jewless Europe and been happy? I don't think so. You would have found another victim and sold them to your people as a different form of a Jew, whether they were a Pole or a Russian or maybe even an Englishman. So what was this all about? Were the Jews the ruination of Germany? How could they be?"

The Jews in Germany consisted of less than one percent of the total population. How could a country with all the intellectuals that Germany possessed turn back to the Stone Age? Suddenly, I was jarred from my thoughts on that fifteenth day of August 1945.

"Attention! Please look out your windows and see the White Cliffs of Dover. Welcome to England."

# Chapter 16

## I am/you are/they are

The British planes plucked us from the ruins of Europe. We saw the destruction over Germany as we flew from Prague. We landed in Crosby-on-Eden and then we were taken to Lake Windemere. It was a whole new world. We seemed so smart and sure of ourselves, but this was only a facade. We were in a new environment and people spoke another language. We all felt very emotional standing on the soil in a free country. We would soon start to grow, not in height, but with knowledge.

We noticed vehicles there, which brought nurses and others to help us. Everywhere we moved people were taking pictures. They led us to the dining room—we occupied the tables and ate for three to four hours. I noticed that I was relatively healthy compared to some. We were housed in various places, which had separate rooms with water, a shower and a bed-sitting area. They were formerly used for RAF barracks. It was wonderful, with carpets, linen and a beautiful view. In these surroundings, with the ghetto and camps behind us, the question was often asked, "Why us … not others?" We undressed and went to sleep.

In the morning we went to the dining hall. We marched because we were not used to walking—we were still in camp drill mode, criticizing each other when we were out of step. As the food was passed, one hundred plates disappeared. We were hiding it. We didn't understand that we would always have what we needed to eat each day. When this was discovered we were told, "Children there is plenty of food, just ask for all you want." After a few weeks we began adjusting to a whole new life. People from all over came to greet us, some were very astute people. We were a novelty in one way, because they had only read about us and had not seen us. Teachers and others came to work with us. The British-Jewish Joint Committee administered everything.

Each part of our lives had to be normalized. Our daily habits needed an incredible amount of modification. We didn't speak English and began learning the basics ... I am /you are/ they are. Rabbi Wise encouraged us to play soccer with him. Everyone supported us. The fear of tomorrow was gradually being replaced with the security of certainty. We knew we would eat, have clothes, shoes and so on. I accumulated five pairs of pants, just to store them away. Someone asked me why I did it and I said, "I won't have any tomorrow." It wasn't long before we started to laugh at ourselves.

The life and habits of the ghetto and the concentration camps slowly began to fade. We had such freedom. One day I swam across the lake. However, I could not stop thinking, "What was our future?" English was difficult to learn compared to Polish. I only had a fifth grade education, no family left and as far as many of us knew, most friends were also gone except for those we met or made in the camps. Eventually we stopped thinking about ourselves only in the context of the past, and began looking to the future. Many of us were sick with dysentery and other things, particularly tuberculosis. The five years of camp life caused many difficulties for us. The question never went away, "Why did we survive?" I couldn't go home any more. Poland was no place to return to. I needed to think ahead.

I was moved to the Cardross Hostel in Scotland. For the train, the trolley, movies etc., we were given some pocket money, but the vendors would not take money from us. "You live there in Cardross? We will not take your money," was the usual comment.

In Scotland, the time spent was similar to England; learning language, studying for trades and adjusting the way we thought about things. Professors from Edinburgh and Glasgow came to tutor us. We had bicycles for transportation around the countryside and worked continuously to learn the language. Some of us wanted to be as proficient as possible, because being seventeen to eighteen years old, we noticed the many beautiful English girls around us—talk about motivation.

# England and Margaret

Eventually, I was moved to Briarfield in Lancashire, England. It was what we would call in the States, a blue-collar town. One night it was snowing, and there was a dance in town. This was eight months after the war. There was a train stopped, and my friends and I could not cross the track. We were going to the dance. There was a girl with a dog, and the leash got wrapped around my leg.

"Now we are one," I joked. We talked and she told me she served in the Army.

"It will be a very nice dance. There will be many nice girls."

"I already found one"

"Who?

"You."

"I have a lot to do."

I invited her to come for a visit sometime where we were staying. I asked her name; it was Margaret. I told her mine was Victor. A few days later she came looking for me in a nice car. We talked, she taught me how to dance and explained that her father owned factories. We said goodnight to each other. She came back again some days later and asked me to go out with her. I was not very confident about myself. The other guys were watching to see how I would respond. We were falling in love. I noticed she was wearing a cross around her neck … I knew I would not get married in England. None of us talked about leaving England at this time. I thought how lucky I was to experience so many things. I was learning to speak English, how to dance and I saved some money because I had a woodworking job. All this was possible because of the British and the British Jews.

*Victor (with tie in front) at Cardross – Margaret (window insert)*

# Chapter 17

## America ... Family ... America

I knew I had two relatives in America. They were my aunts—Hilda and Nacha Yita. At first, I was not so eager to go to America. I wanted to go to Palestine, if I didn't stay in England. However, I wanted my aunts to know that I was alive. As far as I knew, I was the only one of the European Breitburgs who had survived. I wrote to my aunts just like the other boys had done, attempting to make contact with relatives. I sent one hundred postcards to those who might be relatives based on the spelling of names. I sent them to churches and temples etc., saying, "I am alive!"

One Saturday during dinner, the postman came in and began calling out names. I heard Victor Breitburg; once, twice, again and again. As I read the letters I realized I had more relatives in America than I thought. "Dear Victor, come to America; you are the only survivor." In my correspondence, I wrote that I wanted to go to college in England. My aunt responded and told me that there were plenty of good colleges in New York City. In spite of both of these things, I really wanted to go to Israel ... it was very difficult thinking this through.

The day came when I heard my hostel Matron announce, "Victor, congratulations! Your passport has arrived. Now you can leave for the United States any time you desire." She handed me an envelope, which had the seal of the immigration department.

Since I had found my two aunts addresses in New York, and twenty or so cousins, it became a whirlwind life for me. Letters and packages were arriving daily. One of the letters contained a check for $400 to pay for my passage. My two aunts were expecting me to take a plane within a couple of weeks. Was I ready? I was not so sure that I wanted to go to another "Christian" nation? I had heard that there was plenty of anti-Semitism and prejudice in the United States—who needed that. Besides, I had made myself a promise that if I survived I would go to Palestine. Part of the conflict was that I remembered my mother's dream that some day we would reunite with her two sisters and her mother, who were living in Brooklyn. In 1936, all the papers were in order for our family, but our quota number never came up. Now, in 1947, I had the opportunity to go ... I was struggling with which future to pursue. I was happy that I had found my aunts and cousins, because I was no longer alone. I could feel the outpouring of love professed in their writing. To me, America was not the golden Medina any more. I decided to speak to a rabbi and thought to myself, "Maybe he will lead me to the right path?"

The rabbi's answer was simple and direct, "You are now residing in England, and there is not a chance that you will be able to go directly to Palestine. You might go back to Germany, stay in a DP camp, be smuggled out to Italy, board an illegal ship and then sail to Palestine. Most probably, a British ship will intercept you and return you back to Germany. Go to your family in the United States. When Israel becomes an independent country, then you can go, because they will need people like you." I was not happy about it, but he was right.

I started to inquire about airplane accommodations, but was told that there was a waiting list for nine months. It was six months for a ship passage. Things were very busy concerning transportation to America, because the troops were going home, and their war brides were following after them.

While researching my transportation prospects, I was informed that I had won a college scholarship for four years. When I wrote to my aunts about the scholarship, they were concerned and afraid that there might be a conflict with Russia. If I wanted to go to college they said they would support me to go in America. What overwhelmed me about their response was they were afraid that they might lose me. There was also pressure to go to America from my friends, because Palestine was a gamble. They encouraged me so I would not lose my opportunity to start a new life away from war torn Europe.

Mietek Sternfeld had gotten his passport at the same time I did. He approached me and suggested that we travel together. From my research, I knew Liverpool had a commercial port and there might be some small ships that were going to the U.S. We got the Manchester Guardian newspaper every day and scanned it for information so we could make inquiries. Within two weeks we were notified that a ship was sailing on February 10, at 11 A.M. When I told Margaret that it was time for me to leave England, her father offered me a wonderful job. I had a picture of Margaret with this written on the back:

*Dear Victor,*

*If we will be together, I do not know. So many things seem so uncertain in this life, but this I would like to write. Of all the time I spent with you, I enjoyed every moment of that time. When this picture is old fashioned, the world will still be new. That is all I can say, but it is with my whole heart that I say it.*

I was not sure of my feelings for her. I said, "I want to go to America. People are waiting for me there."

The name of the ship was the SS Saint Louis. When we arrived, we discovered it was a freighter, and that it took only five passengers. America called these ships "thirty-two day wonders," because it that is all it took to build them. Sternfeld and I looked at each other. We were quiet for a few moments and then I said, "We are survivors and we are going to endure this voyage. I wonder how many hits this ship took from German submarines?" We both started to laugh. It took three weeks to cross the Atlantic; it was a rough sail. A storm kept us out of port for a few days, which only increased the anticipation of finishing the journey.

When we arrived, I said goodbye to Mietek, and I scurried down the gangplank. I stepped off and I was in America. Aunt Hilda and her children were waiting for me. They recognized me from the photos my Grandma Sura Keila had brought with her from Poland. We all cried, and I said, "I do have a family, I am not alone anymore."

# SECTION FOUR

### *Over The Distances Of Years and Yearnings*[19]

What do you mean?
No longer here?
How could I let it be?
I forfeit my responsibility.
Life is the ultimate game,
At which everyone loses.
Nothing else means anything.
For my heart has died.
And with the passing of the sun,
The world—I care for less.
But God, why?
I feel too alone.
Yet, I shall not go quietly
Into the depths of darkness.
Life did taste so sweet,
And I crave it still.
My fire burns,
Eternal it will last.
They cannot beat me,
Nor shall I be beaten.
I am man and we are one.
Together, unstoppable and strong.

Untitled poem written by Matthew Gonser, after Victor spoke to Mrs. Cohen Willard's 10H English class, at Amityville High School, in April 2000.

---

[19] Tucker, Duane. *Boats of Silver (For Mom), 17*: See www.poetryofthesoul.com.

# Chapter 18

## More Than Trees Grow in Brooklyn

The car stopped at 440 Barbie Street. It was a nice tree lined street and had a typical American suburban look. It was a two-family house, and my aunt proudly said that they were living downstairs. My cousin Phil helped to bring in my suitcase and he bid me good-by. He also told me that he was taking me out on Saturday evening to Chinatown.

"Come Victor, I, want to show you our apartment," my aunt said. She pointed out where her bedroom was and showed me my room. She told me that the other bedroom was her daughter Annie's bedroom. "Do you know that Annie and Bernie got married?" Then she proudly showed me the living room.

We walked into my bedroom and she said, "Please sit down on the bed." She sat down next to me and started to cry. "Victor, you don't know how long I have waiting and longing to see you. I don't know whether you are aware that I had lost a son and my husband when I was very young, and now you are here, and I want you to feel like you are the son that I lost." For a while there was silence between us. I knew that she meant what she had said, but I was not ready to be adopted.

I knew about my aunt Hilda's history from my mother. Hilda was her heroine. She was short, petite and good-looking. Her son had been run over by a horse and carriage while attempting to cross the road. A short time later her husband died and left her with a six-month old girl. Her sister, Nacha Yita, was already in America and had begged Hilda to join her. The plan was, that if she did, both would work together and bring everybody over to America. Their uncle, Ruben Magnus, would help by being a sponsor—he had the means and the money. He owned a department store in San Francisco (his nephew was Rabbi Jehuda Magness). However, there was a catch … she had to get to Hamburg, Germany first, and on her own. It was not an easy task because World War I was raging all over Europe; but she was unwavering in her decision to go.

Within three weeks, with her mother's blessing, she bundled up her infant and headed toward the German border. When she was near the border, she knew that she would not be permitted to cross by either the Russians or the Germans. She decided to do it on her own during the night. She knew that she would need someone to guide her through the forest. Smuggling through the borders was quite common, especially during wartime when people tried to escape the front line battles. It didn't take long for her to find a group that was going to cross the border; but it would cost. She was told where and when to meet them. She was also told the child had to drink some wine to be sedated. During the night she dressed the baby in warm clothes, and at the designated time she gave the baby a small dose of wine. She carried the baby on her back because she wanted her hands to be free.

The group consisted of 20 people, and they were told to spread out and follow the guide. The guide stopped and informed them that they had crossed the border from Poland into Germany. "You are now on your own; watch out for the border patrol." The guide thanked them for the money, told them that within one kilometer there was a village, wished them good luck and disappeared into the darkness of the forest. Everybody went in different directions, when suddenly they heard a command to stop. Every one did except Hilda. She jumped into the ravine, grabbed the black shawl from her back, which covered her baby and instantly she became invisible. After awhile there were no signs that anyone was around. She started walking, but not into that village. She didn't trust the guide. Suddenly there was a single shot. She froze—there was nobody there.

Hilda thanked God the baby was still asleep. She walked another hour and decided to feed the baby. She sat down in the wheat patch, took out her breast, uncovered the baby and prodded the nipple into her mouth. But there wasn't any motion. She panicked and started to shake the baby, to no avail. She undressed the baby and she felt that the baby's clothes were soaked. Then she saw the blood. She screamed to the Almighty, "Why did the baby have to die from a bullet which never was aimed at her?" She continued walking, found a village and asked whether there was a Jewish synagogue. The news rapidly spread about the woman who was walking with a dead baby. Two Jews appeared and took the baby from her. "We will bury the child with our custom." The burial was a day later and the rabbi said Kaddish. A couple of days after that, the village purchased a ticket for her to Hamburg, Germany. In Hamburg she waited for a ship for two weeks, and from there sailed to America. It took nearly eighteen days to get to Ellis Island. Upon arrival, she was released to the custody of her sister.

Nacha Yita brought her to her home. Hilda worked with Nacha Yita in her kosher chicken store. Two years later, she was introduced to a widower, twenty years her senior, who had two small children. They were married and two more offspring were born: Annie and Ida. In 1927, just after I was born, they brought Sura Keila, their mother (my grandmother) from Europe to America, with the hope that sooner or later the whole family would be together. There had been a rift between the sisters that didn't permit them to fulfill their dream. But the sisters reconciled when they found me in England.

In America, I missed Margaret and started feeling miserable. I had been sharing an apartment with my aunt and cousin, but my cousin and I didn't get along very well. One day I told my aunt I was going to visit my aunt Hilda in Manhattan. She wanted me to stay home, but I went anyway. My aunt wanted to send me to college. My cousin and my aunt were arguing when I came home, and I overheard their discussion. "You didn't have money to send me to college but now you have it to send him?"

I felt bad and I pretended I didn't hear them. I told them I had changed my mind about college. I had a job and said I would just keep working. It seemed to relieve the tension. Soon after that, I moved out to a place not far from where I was working. I worked at the Acro Fireplace Factory in Brooklyn, off Pitken Ave. I became friends with many people at work. A fellow worker's mother had a room for me and Mrs. Frishman became my landlady. Her terms were, "I will not cook or do your laundry." She didn't keep her word. Every morning she made me breakfast. "You can't go out without eating," she insisted.

I truly came to appreciate America. I had been making my way in my new country and everyone was incredibly generous to me. This was very important because before coming to America in 1947, I was aware of some American history. I knew about prejudice against blacks and discrimination. I didn't understand what the root of this kind of prejudice was. I saw this as demeaning to what America stood for. All kinds of people, even Jews, were prejudiced. This shocked me. Once, one of my cousins was with me in the playground across the street, relaxing outside and watching the children play. A lady was sitting there and my cousin walked away from her. I asked, "Why?" She said, "I don't like black people." This was Reisal, the one I used to watch over in Kaminsk!

"What is wrong with you Reisal? You spent six years in the camps and I just don't understand how you can think this way." She walked away. We didn't speak for a long time after that.

I saw prejudice all over New York City from so many different kinds of people. Once, in the first four years of being here, and not long after getting married, I thought I would just return to England with my wife. Thank God for Eisenhower and the Brown vs. Board of Education Supreme Court case in 1954. It occurred seven years after I came to America, and four years after I became a citizen. Even though the Civil Rights struggle didn't end there, for me it was a moment of great expectation. When the boys were killed in Mississippi in 1964, I became skeptical and wondered if it was worth Black and Jewish boys risking their lives in the movement? When I saw the water hoses, the beatings and the dogs being let loose on marchers over the next few years, you can only imagine the feelings I had—remembering the brutality of the ghetto and the camps. I also didn't understand the genocide of Native Americans. Having experienced this in my life, it was difficult for me to reconcile some of the contradictions of such a great country. This was troubling, and in spite of what I loved about America, I was disappointed. However, the colonial years of British rule and the treatment of the Irish and the Scots and others, were not jewels in the crown of England's history. By the time Martin Luther King, whom I greatly respected, and Bobby Kennedy were assassinated, I was still uncomfortable, but able to move on, hoping for a better America, as so many others did.

# Chapter 19

## Making My Way

One day a man noticed that I was reading the *New York Times* and he was surprised; I didn't know why. Did I look uneducated or like I was struggling to make sense out of what I was looking at? He said, "How long have you been in this country?"

"Four weeks."

"What did you learn this morning from such a great paper?"

"Many things, but *The Manchester Guardian* is a better newspaper."

I had registered myself for one year of night school at Thomas Jefferson High School. I wanted to learn more about America and other practical things. During an early class, the teacher asked for a volunteer to go and meet with other students to be involved in some social action activities. I said, "What do I know about social action. I have only been here for four weeks. I don't know what you mean?"

"You will do very well. Go and register and I will give you extra points."

I had to make a speech for this group of students; I don't remember the topic. Following the speech, there were nominations for officers for this group. From the other end of the room a woman's voice said, "I am nominating Mr. Victor Breitburg for VP." I walked over to meet her. Her name was Lucille Edelmann. I thought, "Wow, I have been in this country for such a short time and already I am a Vice President. I guess anything is possible."

During the time we were finishing school at Thomas Jefferson, Lucille and I would meet and walk home together. Lucille worked during the day and finished high school at night. Her family could not afford college. Her father was a rather harsh man. Her mother died when she was nine; that attracted us to one another. Having lost our mothers at an early age created a common bond between us. She had a mentally retarded sister. Lucille worked with many organizations that provided services to all kinds of people, and I started to go to with her to those meetings. This was influencing me to see the value of investing some of my life to help meet the needs of others.

At that time, I had been looking for a larger apartment and working in a factory that made store fixtures. A co-worker told me that he lived on the second floor of his building and that the lower was available. He rented the apartment to me and we became friends. There were two salesmen at our company. During the war, one ended up in Germany after being shot down by mistake by the Allies. He married the great granddaughter of the Schiff family, who died on the Titanic, and he was always trying to set me up with women. I was a member of his wedding party. We had a nice friendship.

Going into the third year of seeing Lucille, I was not certain about our relationship and I didn't want to be just dating girls. Margaret and I had lost contact with each other and there was no opportunity to renew that long distance relationship. I liked so much about Lucille. Here, in America, was a girl who was on her own. She worked hard, cared for her sister and maybe we could help one another in life. I was thinking in a rather practical way at that time.

After having a couple of drinks at a Christmas party, I left and decided to buy a present for Lucille. She was a smoker. I bought her a combination lighter/cigarette case. I had it engraved with the letters LB (not LE)—maybe I had more than a couple of drinks. A few months later, I invited her to come on a Saturday to the mountains where I visited my aunt every weekend. When she arrived, I presented her with a very unorthodox, and not a particularly romantic proposal.

Abruptly, I said, "How would you like to get married to me?"

"Real marriage?"

I said to myself, "I didn't know there was any other kind." She was thinking about a formal wedding, not just going to a justice of the peace.

"Yes!"

On June 11, 1949 we got married in the Bristol Temple Jewish Hall in Brooklyn. We paid for our own wedding and invited one hundred guests. My best man was Mietek (Michael) Sternfeld, who sailed with me to America. We had a beautiful wedding and reception, and then we honeymooned in Canada.

117

A Rage To Live

After we were married, we lived in an apartment in Brownsville and later moved to Queens. I was working in the Greenwich Store Fixtures Factory. The Carpenter's Union sent me to Brooklyn Technical College to affirm my skills. In the early days of our marriage we struggled financially like many young newlyweds. Eventually, I was given a different position at my job, and better pay through the union. We started to think about having children. In 1952 I decided to go to night school because someone noticed my interest in technical drawings. He recommended the Pratt Institute. I didn't have a resume of formal education to present with an application, as colleges and technical schools required. However, the man encouraged me, "What have you got to lose?" I went to the school administration and asked if I could enroll. I was asked to take a test because I had no records of my education. I passed and was admitted. I attended for 5 years by way of night school and got my diploma in 1957 for Interior Designing/Drafting, and I also studied people management strategies. Even with those studies, for the rest of my career, I became a production manager instead of a designer.

While I was working and studying, our first daughter was born. I was scared. What did I know about babies? At least I can say I overcame my earlier education in these matters and didn't wait for the Bocian to arrive. On April 18, 1952 a girl was born and we named her Denise. Her middle name was Lee, after my father. When we brought her back from the hospital and laid her down in the crib, we could not take our eyes off her. I never thought I could love someone so much! Does she look like my mother, my sister, my brother Felek, or somebody from Lucille's family? My fears dissipated when I held her in my arms. It was love at first sight—she was the product of both us. I learned to change diapers, how to make and warm formulas by testing it on my hand and how to bathe her. I'm not sure if studying at The Pratt Institute or learning to be a father was more difficult.

I remember her giggling while I washed her in a basin, and she always took the opportunity to get me wet. She took her first steps when she crawled to the little table, stood up, picked up a grape and brought it to me. I used to come home from school at 11 P.M. Lucille would get angry because I would wake up the baby, so that I could spend a little time with her, and she didn't want to go back to sleep. Then I did my homework for school until 1 or 2 A.M. Two and a half years later history repeated itself, and my second daughter, Myra, was born on October 1, 1954. She had blond curly hair, and this time there were more of the traits of the Breitburgs. Now I am 84, and chuckle to see that my daughters have joined AARP.

Life became somewhat easier, our finances were improving and in 1957, we bought our home in Levittown, N.Y. It was not a grandiose house, but because of my design and building experience I had plans for remodeling and additions. The original house was 900 square feet. By the time we sold it and moved to Florida in 2007, the house was 2300 square feet, with many improvements and a large garden.

I was on unemployment for a short time because the Greenwich Factory went out of business. I received my first check and went to the employment office for an interview. I shared my work and education experience. The interviewer said he had a place he thought would be good for me. He prepared an information card.

"Here, go to see Hindsmann and Waldmann."

I was shivering. After suffering under the Germans for six years I could not imagine working for Germans, even if they were Americans. The idea was very difficult for me to reconcile emotionally. I had also heard they were out of favor with the unions.

"You have nothing to lose … go and interview." I still looked hesitant.

"Victor, you don't understand. You must give me a good reason not to go to an interview. Take my word … they are not like the rumors you have heard. You will be very surprised. If you don't like it there, I will check off on your record that it was not a job for you."

When I arrived, I went to the drafting department and showed my drawings to the head draftsman. He called Mr. Hindsmann. When he entered the room I saw a very German looking man with a big cigar, and I laughed as I thought to myself that he could have been an SS officer.

"Mr. Breitburg, how much money do you want for this position?"

"Let me work for three to four weeks for nothing, and let's see if we are compatible with each other. Let me prove myself first, then we can discuss money."

I was hired as the production manager. They were on the third floor of a large building and they made store fixtures. Many employees spoke German, and eventually I got used to it. I knew some German from the years in the camps. After three weeks they gave me a hefty check, and they decided to pay me one hundred dollars per week to start.

"Do you mind if I join the union?" There was no opposition (PS-erase that rumor from memory). A short time later, his production man took sick and I was given that position. Every night my reports were on Mr. Hindsmann's desk. Whatever I recommended, he agreed to. In spite of the promotion, I still had not met Mr. Waldmann.

One rainy day, I had to send some product for delivery. No one wanted to go down and get the elevator to move the product. I knew there was no use in sending a kid from among the workers until we got the material downstairs, so I went down to get the elevator. I cut in front of other people and took the elevator to the third floor to get the product loaded. Two hours later, I was told that Mr. Waldmann wanted to see me. I didn't know where his office was. I found out and went to see him.

In his office, there was a man drinking coffee. He offered me some and asked me, very politely, to sit down and join him. Then he said, "You know, no one has ever done that to me. No one has closed the gate and taken my elevator from me ... after all, I own the building and the business." That was my formal introduction to Mr. Waldmann. I got a bit red in the face, not in anger but in embarrassment. I explained that I had already sent three guys down to get the elevator. "But you don't close the door on the boss."

Then he said, "Ok, let's talk. I am very pleased with your work and so is my partner. You are the first Jewish person we have hired. When I first came to America I hired Germans because I could not speak English." (PS-another rumor squashed.) Let me tell you a short story: "My brother was a communist and was killed by the Nazis. They were looking for me next. I obviously escaped and made my way to this country." I realized we had more in common than I would have ever thought possible. He stood up, shook my hand and said, "You will be an asset to our business."

One night the following week, I was finishing late and only had about an hour to get to school. It was raining and I had not finished some paperwork. Mr. Hindsmann came in and asked me why it would not be completed. I told him about school and that I would finish first thing in the morning.

"But why do you need so much time to get to school. Don't you have a car?"

"No, I don't. I take the train."

"I can help." He called the janitor and signed out a car.

"Use this car for the rest of the school year. Where are you eating dinner?"

"Wherever I can get a frankfurter."

"Look," he said, as he opened up a wallet. "We are not a fly-by night company. We go out to dinner and we order in if need be. I know you are short on time, but use this card and eat whenever you want to … it won't cost you anything."

Over time my job responsibilities grew. One day I saw two guys working, and asked them to do something the way I needed it to be done. By my third request, they were still not responding. I went to the administration office and told them that these men should be let go for not doing proper work. They challenged my authority in front of Mr. Hindsmann, who was not showing them sympathy. They said they were going to complain to the union. I had their final checks in my hand and all I said was, "If you change your attitude, you can come back on Monday."

They looked at each other, nodded and replied, "We'll think about it." They came back and became some of my best workers.

The way the production area was built, people went downstairs to bring up plywood. This was time consuming and added to the cost of the finished product. I mentioned to my bosses that I had an idea about that, and how to make more money. I drew up a design and included time studies for the bathroom vanities they were building. It seemed that production costs were more than they should have been. I showed them to the two salesmen.

"Thirty-five to forty dollars per unit is what you should be getting."

"Did I tell you we were not making money?"

I showed them the calculations right down to the nails.

"We have to raise our prices at least fifteen percent."

One said, "The market won't take it." The other said, "How do you know this?"

"Well, here are the figures."

They told me that other companies were selling them cheaper. I asked, "Do you know if they are the same quality? I went to look at some. They didn't have bottoms or cross supports. The quality is not the same."

After sharing this with the owners, they decided not to lose money on the units, and decided to close that part of the business. The two salesmen heard about this, approached the owners and said they would like to buy the vanity division. They asked me to come along. I said, "If I am not so good at understanding these things and don't know about prices and so on, why do you need me?" There was silence. Then they apologized. I asked, "What are you going to give me?"

"We will offer you ten percent of the business, or ten percent of the business profits and an increase in salary."

Based on this agreement, we began our new enterprise. Eventually, we all went to other companies. After I graduated from the Pratt Institute in 1957, I finally decided to go on my own, building the same kind of product. I started a small business in Lynbrook, on Long Island, New York, with Bill Meyers. Then in 1970, with two friends from the Pratt Institute, Jerry and Joe, we started The Prestige Cabinet Corporation in Freeport, New York.

I was the production manager, Jerry was the office manger and Joe was the salesman. We worked very well with each other, but didn't socialize much because we spent so much time together on the job. We were a union shop with an ethnically diverse work force. We were successful, and after a few years, I realized there had to be a better way to make a quality product at a cheaper cost. I began to investigate computerized machinery for cutting pieces from templates in bulk. Our cabinets were high quality, pre-fabricated vanities and wall units and some had glass components.

My partners asked me to explain what I wanted to do. I told them I wanted to go to Los Angeles for a trade show promoting new technology that would help us. They agreed. When I got there, I asked the sales representative to give me a quote as to how much it would cost with this new equipment, to produce a particular number of pieces. I called my partner Jerry and he said, "I am not interested in your toys, just tell me the cost."

"$890,000." He hung up.

I was laughing and knew he would call back. Thirty minutes later he did. I explained, in detail, what the machines could do to save labor costs, and I guaranteed that we would do $2,000,000 more in sales in one year if we purchased the equipment. I explained, "It takes three people to cut a panel: one man to place it on the machine, one to cut it and one to carry it away. With the equipment we could do a bundle (thirty six panels) in 1.5 hours." Once we began the new computerized system, with proven results, we added drill machines, screwing machines and others as needed. In the first year we made close to $3,000,000; we had eighty-one employees and office staff.

Running your own business, even a partnership, always has its ups and downs. You are going to be involved with your employees in one way or another, more than owners might be in a larger corporation. One day I received a call on the in-factory line. It was my foreman, Mike. "Mr. Breitburg, may I come to your office for a short discussion?"

"Yes." I knew that he would not call me that early in the morning unless it was important.

"Mike, sit down. Would you like a cup of coffee? What is the problem?"

"Mr. Breitburg, Leo Fernandez hasn't shown up for work the last three days, and as you know this is not the first time it has happened. I have decided that we have to fire him." I agreed that the decision was right and I had to back up my foreman.

"Did you clear it with the shop steward?"

"Mr. Breitburg, I was waiting for your approval." Normally he never needed my permission, but he knew how I felt about Leo.

"Mike, go and tell the shop steward about your decision. Take him into the office and don't forget to call the union. I don't want any problems. Then call me back."

After he left I thought about Leo. He had worked for me for the last five years. What had happened to him? I remember when he came into my office asking for a job. He was well dressed and highly recommended by one of my employees. Reading his application, I found out that he came from El Salvador. He was a high school graduate. His wife and daughter were still living in El Salvador. I asked Leo why they remained behind.

"Within three years I will bring them over to the United States. By that time I will have an apartment all furnished, and my daughter will be finished with medical school in Salvador."

Leo was a dynamo. He worked in my place for 48 hours per week, and was also employed evenings, cleaning offices. Once in awhile, after hours, he would clean my office, and show me pictures of his family and apartment. Over a period of time there was a change in Leo. I noticed this, and asked Mike what was happening. He informed me that Leo's apartment had been burglarized, twice, and that he had lost most of his possessions. The civil war in El Salvador was also making it impossible for him to get into the country to see his family.

After instructing Mike to make the phone call, I contacted Leo and asked him to have dinner with me, thinking I could be of some assistance. He looked helpless and lonely. I asked him how he felt. For a while he was silent, and then he started to speak up, "Mr. Breitburg, you were always kind to me and I do appreciate it. I live in a ghetto surrounded by killings and drugs. I cannot hold on to anything. I have tried to get out from there, but being black and Latino is not easy. I have to support my family in Salvador. Maybe I will go back to Salvador."

The evening ended on a sad note. I remember when I came to the United States from England. I didn't experience what many immigrants have to go through. I spoke English, I had job training and I had relatives who were very supportive.

The next morning the factory line rang. "Yes."

"Mr. Breitburg, this is Mike … the union gave us permission to discharge Leo Fernandez."

My stomach was churning, but I had to do it. I rang the human resources office and asked for Ms. Carroll, our payroll accountant. I instructed her to mail Leo a discharge letter and a check for any payroll and vacation money, which might be due, but not less than one week of vacation pay. This was the most difficult time I ever had releasing an employee, especially such a good worker.

I was beginning to think about retiring in the mid-eighties. We had already purchased a condo at Wynmoor Village in Florida, spent some time there and rented it out. My daughter Denise had married Mark Smith. We became grandparents when Maya Sarah Breitburg-Smith was born on April 13, 1983. The blessing was repeated when Eli Breitburg-Smith was born on July 18, 1987.

October 19, 1987 was Black Monday, and the stock market crashed. The world was in trouble. We were losing contracts. My family urged me to retire and I did. I didn't take any money from the company at retirement. I had saved and invested during my career. For thirty years I had successful businesses. Two years later, Prestige closed its doors.

*Victor and Lucille-Wedding and Anniversary*

*Maya*     *Mark  Eli*     *Denise*        *Myra*

## Born To Be a Traveling Man

When the girls were small we visited the usual spots in New York State like Santa Clause Village and Lake George. Once we were traveling and stopped at a chalet and saw people on snowmobiles. We decided to give it a try. It took control of us and we were all over the place. It eventually stopped as it turned over. We were not injured because of all the snow. It was great fun. Lucille watched from the sidelines.

I loved skiing. I learned to ski in Zakopane, Poland, on the Czech border, with my father. In 1979, my daughter Denise called from California and asked if we would like to go skiing. What kind of question was that? "Lets go!" I said. We booked our tickets and off we went for a week of skiing at Mount Mammoth in California.

When we arrived at the airport, Denise and Mark (my future son-in law) were already waiting, and we went to Mount Mammoth. Denise had reserved a Swiss style chalet for us. After dinner we settled down at the fireplace and were chatting. I asked about what type of skiing we would do. Skiing on new terrain is like driving on a new highway with a brand new car for the first time. I wanted to be prepared. "I hope that we will have enough snow, after all it's mid May," I said.

Denise started to laugh, "Dad, they ski here until mid August. You're going to ski on six feet or more of snow." I didn't want to ask any more stupid questions and I said goodnight. I went up the curved stairwell, which led directly through the floor to our bedroom. The bedroom had three walls and the front was a three-foot partition and a rail. Sitting on the bed I was looking at the beautiful curved window, which started two feet from the floor and extended up to the ceiling.

The next morning, as soon as I awoke, my eyes were riveted at the panoramic view of the mountains. Within one hour, Denise, Mark and I were ready to leave. "Go, I'd rather stay in this nice warm cozy room than be cold on the outside," Lucille said.

We packed our equipment in the car and off we went. Within thirty minutes I had my ski boots on and was standing and gazing at the mountain. Now I was having second thoughts. "Denise, how tall is this mountain?"

"14,000 feet above sea level."

"I did not ask you for sea elevation."

"It's about 8,000 … are you chickening out?"

"Oh no, but I see that condos are going up, and then they disappear into heaven. Do those people ever come back?"

"C'mon dad, you taught me how to ski. You can do it."

On the way up on the ski lift, I noticed that some condos were empty, and told Denise that all the people who were in them must be in heaven already. After a while we stopped and disembarked. I told Denise and Mark to go on with out me and that I would catch up with them. I really wanted them to go, because I wanted to spend some time alone with my thoughts. I put on the skis, zipped up my zippers, tightened my belt and went to the tip of the starting point. I looked around. If anybody does not believe that there is a God, let this person come up on Mount Mammoth. The panoramic view was breathtaking.

Some years later I got interested in diving. Denise was already diving as a marine biology student, and I thought it might be nice to dive with her one day. Lucille and I took a trip to the Caribbean. I saw an instructor and asked him how much it would cost for a lesson. Once I had my tank and mask on, and learned the breathing, I thought that was it. The instructor said, "Now you get to go in the ocean." He took me out for a dive and I had great fun swimming with the fish. Denise told me that if I liked diving I should take more instruction. I joined a diving school on Long Island and learned more skills and safety/rescue procedures. We visited Denise in California and I went diving with her while she was doing a project for her studies concerning some particular fish on the reefs. On a visit to Israel, I was also able to dive. After a few years I gave it up because my ears started to bother me. However, loving horses the way I do, I could still go riding whenever possible.

We visited much of America. I know we never went to Iowa, Nebraska, Kansas, Oklahoma or Alaska. After I retired, we traveled a bit more. Our later travels took us to France, Morocco, Egypt, Israel, Greece and the Islands, Italy, Spain and Portugal. England, Denmark, Sweden, and Holland also made the list. In 1996 I visited Poland and the Czech Republic for the first and only time since the war had ended. We never made it to the Far East.

I made my first trip to Israel n 1969, after I attended a "Boys" reunion in England.

Lucille did not want to come at that time because the War of Attrition with Egypt was still going on. I stayed at Krulik's home for two days and then at Balsam's home until I left for Israel. My friend, Tulek Rosenschweig was waiting for me to come.

I took a tour of Israel that year and had not planned on staying in many homes. I wanted to see as much of Israel as possible in a twelve-day tour, although I visited for longer than that. Some of the boys came along on the trip and we had a bit of a celebration and they made sure that each night we visited someone and spent time together.

As a young boy I was always taught about Israel. I went to Jerusalem, Masada and many other sites. This was a country of Jews who were not afraid of their enemies, and I had not witnessed any prejudice against Christians or Muslims. However, I was very troubled about Israel and the political climate at the time. The soldiers were always armed in the streets and on watch seven days a week.

In Jerusalem I visited the Christian sites like Mary's Well, the church with the stairs where Jesus was said to have walked, and I prayed for Israel at the Wailing Wall. I prayed for their survival. I was on the top of the mountain in a hotel and had a view of all of Jerusalem, Masada, and the Dead Sea.

I went to visit a new town that was being built and I was a bit angry because they had good quality wood and it was just setting on the ground, unprotected. I saw more waste than I thought I would since the country had been around for twenty-years. I saw a man who had good machinery, but he was not utilizing it to its full capabilities. Then I saw good mahogany lying on the ground. It seemed that the people were just too preoccupied with the war and the current political climate.

It was a wonderful 24 days. Friends from Scotland and England were with me.

The first time I visited, the airport was very basic. My next trip was a completely different experience. I saw new high-rise buildings, and Tel Aviv was now a modern city. Each of my seven trips, some with Lucille, showed more of the progress of the Jewish people in Israel.

On one trip I was able to dive in the red sea and it was just beautiful. One day I went to swim and did not wear my sandals; the sand was so hot on my feet, that when I entered the water, I saw the steam rising from my toes.

I even spoke with some Arabs on one of my trips. Then I decided I wanted to visit Egypt on my next trip. You will see so many different things there. I had to touch all kinds of things in the landscape and thinking that perhaps some of my ancestors had walked through some of these places. Of course things in Egypt today are different right now with the Arab Spring, but once things are secure again you should take the trip if you can. The most fun was just talking with so many different people. Young children loved watching me take pictures and seeing how a long lens camera is used.

I believe the Palestinians should have a separate state. Peace should be attainable. The co-existence of Israel and Palestine could mutually benefit the entire Middle East and I hope that one day, there will be a true peace between those peoples.

In 1975, I went to London and Israel with Lucille. It was so wonderful to see those who survived along with me being so full of life, albeit a few were getting a little chubby but it was still easy to recognize everyone. In some ways many had changed more than others, but the eyes were the same. Among them there was a dentist, a professor and Ben Hefglott, a businessman and Olympic Champion for England. Ben is one of the organizers of our reunions, and has served as chairman of the '45 Aid Society.

A guy with a wig and a cane welcomed the boy from the States. They brought a big cake for my birthday, May 8, Liberation Day and the weekend we have our reunions. They called me Schlamic. I was overwhelmed, but I did not cry. I was blessed by how I was welcomed, Lucille said, "We are coming next year too!"

Our meetings last for one and a half days and then some go to Israel. It was a big affair. Krulik provided the sightseeing for those from outside of England, and we were so busy, that sometimes we didn't eat. That is a bit ironic, recalling how we had hidden plates of food at Windemere when we first arrived in England after the war. We were active during the entire stay, and the hospitality was superb. Memories were always being shared. In the camps we all had partners for survival; no one could have made it on their own.

Then we went to Israel to visit the boys who lived there. England was the hub for the gathering and then it was off to Israel. People from Israel came to London and then back again to Israel. In Israel, we always stayed in the homes of friends. Over the years the families of "The Boys" began attending the reunions. The camaraderie is still like that today. Today there is a group formed from the '45 Aid Society called the Second Generation. The families of "The Boys" are carrying on the traditions of the original society.

Many of "The Boys" are gone now. Those who can, stay in contact by phone, but physically gathering is getting more difficult. I have attended four or five reunions over the years. A few of us live here in Florida.

# Chapter 20

## A Memorial, A Torah Cover and Christmas

There are four things of particular significance that I was involved with during the years of my retirement before moving to Wynmoor: continuing to lecture about the Holocaust until 2005, helping to build a Holocaust Memorial at The Suburban Temple, working on a committee for a Holocaust Torah Cover and helping to establish a food distribution during Christmas from our Temple.

In 1987, the President of The Suburban Temple, Morton Held, was presiding at the congregational board meeting. On the agenda for discussion was the feasibility of building a Holocaust Memorial. It was noted that I was the Vice President, a Holocaust survivor, and that I had outlined the necessity of such a project along with the need to form a Holocaust committee. At this time, the issue of cost and design was not discussed. A motion was made and a short discussion followed. Rabbi Raab impressed everyone with a short commentary of approval. The motion was unanimously passed.

Morton Held and I decided that we would co-chair the committee. Within a couple of weeks a committee was established with approximately fifteen temple members joining in, and the first meeting was held. The criteria for our mission was: (1) Type of a Holocaust Memorial and where it should be placed (2) A garden adjacent to the memorial should be considered (3) Place to be chosen should be in the front of the Temple (The reason for the garden was a place for reflection) (4) To get a designer from the outside of our temple in order to minimize criticism (5) How much money will have to be raised (6) Will we get any money from the temple treasury. A decision was made that the Holocaust committee would meet once a month until the completion of our mission.

At our next meeting the agenda was: (1) A vote from the congregation was needed (2) A stipend of money had to be given to start the project (3) Each family had to contribute ten dollars toward the memorial. If the congregation would not approve the memorial, then everything else was moot.

At our May congregational budget and election meeting, the agenda was put forth. I was called up to explain the necessity of a Holocaust Memorial. A long line of people lined up at the microphone to speak. The questions asked were: Do we need a Holocaust Memorial? Can we afford a memorial when our roofs are leaking, and other necessities needed? How much will it cost, $75,000, $100,000 etc.? Where is it going to be placed? All the questions were thoroughly answered. The congregation was reassured that it would be less than $50,000, and that most of the money would come from voluntary contributions from within the temple and from the community. Each temple family would have to contribute ten dollars. Having over 600 families, that would give us $6,000 to begin with. We also would ask the congregation for the approval of the design. If the design was approved, and the cost was not prohibitive, then the building of the memorial would commence. Rabbi Raab and Morton Held spoke on behalf of the project. The congregation approved the building of a Holocaust memorial according to these terms.

By the end of 1988, we had already interviewed four different designers. Each of the designs was unique. They were nice for a museum, but not for the front of our temple. We were looking for a memorial with a message, not a picture of concentration camps. Also, the prices were way over our budget. They ranged from $60,000-$120,000. The committee felt that we had to follow a different path, and invite other designers. I decided to do some sketching on my own to show some ideas to our future designers. At our next Holocaust committee meeting it was shown as an idea only. Not only did the committee like the proposed drawing, a decision had been made to use it as our memorial design. The design was quite simple. It had a wall built with short logs to represent the railroad ties, which brought the Jews to the concentration camps. The Star of David, from which one third is broken away, except at the bottom where a little bit is joined together, represents the loss of one third of all the Jewish population. The little piece joined on the bottom represents the Holocaust survivors. The star was inscribed with the names of each of the camps that had crematoriums, and the number of people who perished there. The wall would be built on an angle with six steps for lighting candles on Yom HaShoa.

A member of our committee, Karl Heiman, had been given the task to come up with a sentence to be placed on the wall. After much research, the final sentence was submitted and approved:

# They Perished Because of The World's Indifference - Never Again

Bids were submitted for the garden and the memorial, and we were quite sure that it could be done for under $40,000, if I was the general contractor. Barbara Held was put in charge of developing the garden and hiring a qualified designer.

The design and the expenditure estimates were given to our new temple President, Regina White, for board and congregational approval. The Temple board and congregation approved the design with a provision that we would not spend more than what was submitted. A check of $6,000 was put into the Holocaust committee account to be used, but more funds had to be obtained.

At our next meeting we proposed a series of six lectures to be held once a week at our temple. The community was invited, and the first one was held two months later. The first speaker was Karl Heiman. He told the story of his youth and schooling under the Nazi regime from 1933 until 1939. Then I described my story, from 1939 in the Ghetto Lódz, Auschwitz, Buchenwald, Rehmsdorf and finally liberation by the Russians on May 8, 1945 at Theresienstadt. The next speakers were two young women. Evelyn Rakos and Helen Jones were interned in Krakow, and had worked at the Schindler factories. In the following weeks, Jean Shissler spoke. She was a second-generation member, whose parents spent time in various camps. After her, there was Janine Berg and her sister. A Christian family hid Janine at the age of two, and the other two sisters were hidden at a Catholic convent in France. The final speaker was an American soldier who liberated Dachau.

Each of the speakers was a temple member. The temple and the community were very supportive with their attendance and contributions of money. I designed a special plaque for the purpose of raising funds for the memorial. The total cost of the memorial and the garden was less than $30,000, and all the money was there before the first shovel went into the ground. The memorial and the garden were dedicated on April 22,1990 under the direction of our new President, Sam Abraham. The initial $6,000 stipend was returned to the temple.

The Holocaust committee is still very active in retaining the garden and the Holocaust Memorial. They support many Holocaust centers throughout the United States, and children who want to participate in the *March Of The Living*. The committee established and bought books for a section of the temple library for the education of future generations.

The Holocaust committee is currently working as hard as we did in the beginning. As older members are no longer with us, new and younger people are joining in to preserve what has become a binding pride in our temple. I say thank you to all the people who made this possible over the years.

# The Holocaust Torah Cover

The Holocaust Torah cover was a three-year project from 1998-2001. Dr. Mel Goldstein and Allan Itzkowitz were the co-chairs of the committee. It was brought to our attention that the Holocaust Torah needed to be repaired. Some of the writing was fading away and some parchments had to be banded, therefore the Torah was not kosher. The Sisterhood undertook to finance the cost of the Torah's repair. The

Torah was over one hundred years old and was discovered in Czechoslovakia. It was rescued from the Nazis and brought to Westminster, England for safekeeping. Some time in the 1960's, The Suburban Temple became the guardian of the Torah. During the meeting, the Holocaust committee suggested that we should obtain a symbolic cover for the Holocaust Torah. I was chosen by the committee to oversee the project. Having the confidence of the Holocaust committee, and a budget not to exceed $2000, I began the search for a Torah cover.

There were several possibilities of pre-made covers, but none expressed what we were looking for. The decision was made to consider an original design. The search extended from Israel to Lynbrook, New York. Even then we believed that we were on the wrong path. Months of research led us nowhere. So, I set up the criteria for the messages that we wanted the Holocaust cover to express.

The cover had to include:

1.  The word Zachor—Remember.

2.  The Talit—In the worst times, whether it was in the ghettos or in the concentration camps, we prayed to the Almighty for deliverance.

3.  The unknown faceless camp uniform—Most of our people thought they were going to take a shower; instead they were murdered by gas.

4.  Our own Holocaust Memorial—The logs represent the railroad ties that took us to the concentration camps. The broken star represents the loss of one third of world Jewry (6,000,000).

5.  The Garden—It represents life. We should never forget that we must create a better world for our children, and for all the future generations. We need to look at the beauty of life, how precious it is, and, teach our children to be tolerant of people who are different than we are.

6. The Holocaust Memorial message—"THEY PERISHED BECAUSE OF THE WORLD'S INDIFFERENCE - NEVER AGAIN" (coined By Karl Heiman).

Now that the criteria were established, I started to prepare some sketches and invited an artist friend, Richard Weilheimer, who was a Holocaust survivor, to help. After the subject had been brought up, he was very reluctant to paint a Holocaust subject. After explaining that the importance of the Holocaust Torah Cover was for future generations, Mr. Weilheimer agreed to do the cover as a favor. Eleven months later the painting was ready, and was encased in a mock up Torah. The painting was truly a beautiful piece of art.

The painting was presented to the Holocaust committee for approval. After displaying the painting, the Holocaust committee approved it and gave permission to go ahead with the project.

Now we had to find someone to transfer the painting onto the cover. We interviewed several embroiderers. Each one had most of the qualifications, but we also needed someone who could paint. We chose a member of our Temple, Barbara Held. Barbara had won many awards for painting, embroidery and various forms of stitching. Her work had been exhibited in many museums, and we were delighted that she was willing to undertake this important task. The last hurdle, and not a surprise to anyone, was to raise the money to pay for it. I turned to Deanna Pasternak, the Educational Director of our religious school, for help. Without any questions, she offered herself to take on the responsibility.

After nine months, the Torah Cover was finished. To say that it was finished would be to minimize what Barbara went through—nine months of heart wrenching ripping, sewing and obsessions. As the Cover was coming along, so was her obsession of love for the work and fear as to whether or not it would be perfect.

On November 9, during the Kristallnacht Service, Rabbi Gale announced that the Czechoslovakia Holocaust Torah was made kosher, and the special Holocaust design for the Torah Cover would be previewed that night. When the Arc door was opened, we were all astounded at the message the Cover communicated to all of us. The Holocaust Cover was officially dedicated on Yom HaShoah, 2001 by the children of The Suburban Temple Religious School. It will be viewed and admired for generations to come.

# Christmas at the Temple

It may sound surprising that Christmas was celebrated at our temple, but hunger never takes a vacation. Twenty-four fellow congregants and I began a tradition that continues to the present day.

I met Mike Moran in 1988. In 1983 he founded the Interfaith Nutrition Network or INN. It is a Long Island-based charity that operates homeless shelters and soup kitchens. I was looking for another outlet for our Temple to be engaged in the community where there was a need. We promoted mitzvah projects dedicated to the Judaic idea of "Tikkun Olam" (healing the world). Other outreaches included blood drives and clothing distributions.

I believed, rather naively, that no one knew how many homeless there were on Long Island—that is until I met Mike. I invited him to speak to our congregation and Mike "woke us up." Soon after his talk we formed a council on social action. One of our efforts was to staff the INN soup kitchens on days it would normally be closed, like Thanksgiving and Christmas. Christmas is such a busy time for many people, and there are not always people available on Christmas Day to give comfort to those who are alone and have nothing.

We served meals at the Mary Brennan Soup Kitchen in Hempstead. It was set up like a buffet and we invited the guests to come in as soon as they arrived and promptly served them juice and salad before the rest of the meal. We did not want anyone waiting outside in the cold. The dinner was usually glazed ham, sweet potatoes, and broccoli. Dessert was cake, fruit and cookies, along with tea or coffee. I would type out a program for the event that listed the menu, as well as the post-prandial activities: "Give out all the presents to the children, give leftover food to people who have families at home, and wish everyone a Merry Christmas and a Happy New Year."

Today, there are a total of 19 soup kitchens, operating as part of The INN network across Long Island. More than 7,500 people are fed each week and Temple B'Nai Torah is still participating each year.

Ever since I was liberated, people have been there to support me and that is why I am who I am today. There really isn't much distance between the prosperity I have known and the needs of others who have very little. They should be treated with respect and dignity, regardless of their circumstances.

# Chapter 21

## The Return To Lódz

For several years I yearned to go back to Poland. I debated with myself to find a reason for doing it. My return, after my liberation, had left me bitter. What I really wanted to do was show my wife, Lucille, a little bit of my heritage. I also wanted to share my experiences in Poland by visiting Lódz and Auschwitz, and other places I had been transported to before leaving for England, after the war.

Many of our "Boys" went back with their families to share their ethnic heritage. Several of my friends were still bitter against the Polish people, for in their experience, no Poles had helped them during the war. Moniek Goldberg, my cousin Harry and others couldn't understand why I would go to Poland and spend money there. After consulting with Lucille, we decided to take a tour, and spend five days in Lódz.

During the entire trip, I wore a yellow Star of David pin on my lapel, from the Wiesenthal Foundation, so that whoever talked to me would know that I was Jewish. My anger hadn't subsided … I had a chip on my shoulder. I was not the same person who had stood at the station in Krakow in 1945. From September 9 to October 9, we visited Prague, Poland and Riga, Latvia. We landed in Warsaw, and transferred to our plane for Prague. After eleven hours of traveling, we arrived in Prague and were met by an elderly gentleman. I conversed in Polish and his reply was in Czech, yet each of us understood the sense of what the other was saying. As we entered the hotel, I commented that it looked familiar. We were ushered to our room, which was too small to stay in for six days. We went down to complain to the consignor. I mentioned that I was in the hotel fifty-one years ago. He stated that there had been a movie theater next door. It was, by coincidence, that we picked the same hotel. After hearing what I said, he gave us a suite for the same price.

The next day we started to revisit the places where I had walked. Our hotel was situated on Wlaclawska, which is right in the center of town, and in walking distance to the historic old town. Prague is a city of renaissance buildings, magnificent bridges, churches that have clocks from every century, palaces with gardens and Jewish recorded history dating back to the 11th century. The first thing we wanted to see was the Jewish heritage of Prague. We visited the ghetto, which dates back to the 13th century, and the temple where legend says that the Golem, who protected the Jews from pogroms, was built on the second floor. It is the oldest temple in Europe. Everything we saw in Prague was the oldest, including the cemetery that has over 100,000 Jewish graves dating back to the 14th century. Prague was supposed to have been preserved by the Nazis as a museum of "Race," meaning nothing was to be destroyed from the former Jewish ghetto. We went to the opera (Othello), and to the national museums.

On the way to Theresienstadt, the camp where I had been liberated, the guide on the bus had heard some of my story and asked if I knew a Mr. Wilder from England. He had been on the same tour less than two weeks ago with twenty-two people, eight of whom were Holocaust survivors. This group was made up of my friends from England. The group is called the '45 Aid Society. They raise money to aid children, which is repayment for the help they had received after the war in England. I didn't recognize too much of Theresienstadt, because I had been confined in a special holding area. Amazingly, the guide brought us to the place called the Hamburger Kasserene, where I had been housed when the Russians liberated us. After this, we left Prague and arrived at the Forum Hotel in Warsaw, on September 15. The hotel standards were as good as any American hotel. Our tour started the next day.

As we checked into the hotel for the first night, people were registering in the lobby for a conference on the SHOA. It was a European Educators Conference with participants from fourteen Eastern European countries, on how to teach the SHOA (Holocaust). The first meeting was being held that evening. I was invited because I lectured to teachers and students regarding the Holocaust. The Polish Minister of Education led the conclave, which included the Ambassador of Israel, a Polish professor from the Lyceum of Paris and a representative from the Jewish World Congress.

The Minister spoke first, about how important it was to remember the Jews who lived in Poland for 1000 years, and how great their contributions were. He felt sad, and guilty, that Poles didn't do more during the war to help Jews, but emphasized that there were Polish people who paid with their lives hiding and saving Jews. Next, the professor from France spoke about the time Jews and Christians lived in peace and harmony and said, "The Jewish nation in Poland had over three million Jews." He kept referring to the Jews as a nation within Poland, over and over again. This upset me.

When the time for questions came I spoke up, "My father fought for the independence of Poland in the First World War, was wounded and received a medal of valor for the battle of Tarnepole. He was an officer in the reserve in the Polish Cavalry. I was born in Poland, and I am a survivor. I have always considered myself to be a Polish national; that is what my passport says. By considering the Jews as a separate nation, the Polish people had never accepted Jews as nationals, and from this type of thinking, anti-Semitism grew until there was a division between Jews and Poles." He thought for a moment and said the way he had expressed it was wrong. He had never thought about it before, and would not use the phrase again.

In the morning, unexpectedly, we met three of my friends from England. They were staying at our hotel. In the afternoon we went to the area that had been the ghetto. Now, it is a memorial within the square. The Mordhai Memorial commemorates the resistance of the 1943 ghetto. This was the first uprising in Europe; they lost, but their heroism is remembered.

We toured Poland for the next fifteen days. Our tour began with a half-day tour of Warsaw. Part of the visit included the Old Town (completely rebuilt as it was before it was completely destroyed by the Germans), the parks, the palaces and the Warsaw ghetto area. We were left off at the Warsaw Jewish Museum. I had hoped to obtain some documents from their archives. To my surprise, we found many original letters written by my uncle to different towns in 1941, asking help for the Jewish residents. He was the Elder of the town, and we were able to trace his existence to 1942. We also found my name on the list of survivors, and that I later went to England. As far as I know, I am the only survivor from Kaminsk. Underneath my name on the survivors list, was listed Brajtburg, Sara-born 1939-gone to Pietekow. This was my sister's information, except for the residence. Tracing this child, all the information mentioned Pietekow, but never Lódz, made me curious.

About one week before the trip, my daughter Denise received a message from a young man in Georgia who found her name on the Internet. He contacted her because their names were so similar; he assumed they were related. She consulted me. We received an email from his father in St. Louis, and his uncle who also resides there. When we came home, I discovered that this Sara lived in St. Louis, and I made a call. She is a distant cousin. As it turned out, these two men are first cousins of my father. Their father and my grandfather were brothers. We planned to visit them. We spell our name Breitburg, and they spell their name Braitberg. Their spelling is from the European spelling. We were told the family originated in Austria, some went to Germany (therefore our German name), and some went to Poland. This part of the family survived the war because they left Poland early, and fled to Russia.

The entire trip was enjoyable, but mainly because we set out to trace our roots. It was successful, except for two incidents. In my birthplace of Kaminsk, I wanted to see my grandfather's grave, but the town had been rebuilt. It was larger and a housing development had been built over the cemetery. Anything proving the previous existence of Jewish heritage there had disappeared. I obtained my father's birth certificate and mine, as well as some other documents pertaining to his birth and his father's birth. Because my father was born in 1902, his documents were in Russian. I was also searching for the records of my father's trial for smuggling, and where my father had been imprisoned for nine months. The man in this office worked overtime to try to help me. He took my address, stating that he would send me any information he found, and he did.

I purposely asked people on the street, from different age groups, for directions to Jewish offices, temples and any Jewish heritage places, in order to see their reactions. Everyone was cordial and many wanted to escort me. Before the war, if a Jewish person had asked a Pole such a question, he might have been told to find the place by himself. The main purpose was to see whether I would encounter any anti-Semitism … I didn't. There were not many older people here, and most of the young people had not encountered any Jews.

# A Rage To Live

In Krakow, while visiting a Jewish museum, a Priest came in with a group of high school students. They had traveled 400 miles to visit the Jewish museum, and probably other places of Jewish interest. The youths recorded my history during the war and asked me why it had taken fifty years for me to return to Poland. I bluntly told them that I had come back right after the war, to Krakow, and found leaflets declaring that Jews should leave Poland and go to Palestine. Poland was the only nation after the war that killed Jews and forced them to leave. The Priest also wanted me to recite the Kaddish for the victims of WWII. Ironically, in the museum at this time, was a Jewish woman, who now lives in New York, who was rescued as a child by a Polish family; the husband was shot for hiding Jewish children.

Every town in Poland has places where there were once Jewish ghettos. Here and there you can find evidence that Jews existed in those places; it helps to encourage Jewish tourism. The streets are narrow cobblestone, and every town has what's called The Old Town. Prince Zamoisk once ruled over this region, and named many places for his family. The town of Lublin was once the seat of the Hasidic movement in Galicia, Poland.

From Lublin, we went to the Majdanek Concentration Camp. The markers tell how many Poles died there, without stating that forty percent were Jews. I protested and told them that there were many nations that perished there, listing Gypsies, Russians, Czechs, etc. The forty percent should have been listed, so that the children of the future would understand the true, historic tragedy of Nazism. I didn't mince any words and I said what I believed to be true. In the next town we visited we encountered the same thing.

Zamosh was a small town where Jews had lived since the 14th century. Sometimes the Jews were the majority and at other times the Catholics. These shifts in population went on for centuries. Writers at one time resided here and described the village life and its beauty. The first thing we asked was where the Jews had lived. We were told that the only thing left was a Jewish synagogue, which at present, was being used as a public library.

After exploring the town, we visited the local museum and found a lot of information about the town's history. We spent about an hour looking for any Jewish references and found none. Knowing very well it wouldn't really matter or make any difference, I had to speak up. I requested to talk to the director of the museum. The docent asked if he could be of any help. Before I finished, the docent replied that his superior needed to answer my question. He was summoned. After listening to what I had to say, his reply was that he could not find any artifacts of Jewish life in Zamosh. At that point, people started to listen in as I told him how easy it would be to go to homes where Jews used to live and ask them for any Jewish artifacts. I gave him the business card from the Minister of Education. I told him that he would be able to get enough Jewish relics to fill the museum if none could be found. I walked out leaving him with the card in his hand … looking rather foolish.

Our next stop was Auschwitz. I recognized some places, including Block 12, my barrack. When we arrived in Birkenau, I pointed out the exact spot where I had been separated from my family, never to see them again. I got a copy of my entrance and departure cards from Auschwitz and Theresienstadt, because the Germans kept impeccable records. After returning to Warsaw, we immediately got first class tickets and made ourselves comfortable for our journey to Lódz. As the train left the Warsaw station, my anticipation started to grow. I began to tell Lucille things about Lódz like, "In 1939 the population of Lódz was 660,000 and the Jewish population was 225,000. The first things you will see are the tall chimneys. We are going to stay in one of the most beautiful hotels in Lódz, and you are going to see the beautiful stores on Piotrkowska Street."

The train was picking up speed and within a couple of minutes we passed the outskirts of Warsaw. I was glued to the window trying not to miss anything, and once again I was a little kid, as if time had stood still. We saw a woman picking up potatoes in a field with her bare hands. We saw a farmer plowing with a horse. I felt excited as my eyes were trying to drink in the view. After three hours we arrived in Lódz. Where were the chimneys? We took a taxi, and with a commanding voice I told the driver to take me to the Grand Hotel. Within ten minutes we were there. As I looked around, nothing was the same as I remembered it. On parts of Piotrkowska Street the lights were out, and the street was partly broken up.

"Are you sure we are at the Grand Hotel?"

"Yes sir."

I used to walk from the station past the hotel down to Plac Wolnosci. I remembered that it used to be much further. I was told before our trip, "Don't go back … you *will* be disappointed."

My suitcases were deposited on the sidewalk. I paid the driver and gave him a hefty tip so he would not say that Jews are cheap. He could not thank me enough. We were ushered into our room, but it didn't look as luxurious as I had expected. I was judging the place as an American tourist. We decided to leave our suitcases in the room and take a walk down Piotrkowska Street to Plac Wolnosci. I wanted to show my wife so many of the things I had spoken about—the glitter and the beauty of the city at night. We walked slowly and I was getting upset. I asked myself, "Where are the bright lights? Where are the stores?" Lódz was not bombed. The Germans didn't destroy this city. It was as if I heard the street saying to me, "I also suffered." This street was a part of my childhood, and my emotions were hanging on my sleeves.

I remembered when I asked my mother for permission to show my little brother Felek this street. I held on to his hand, and showed him the stores and explained all the new things displayed. We passed the Grand Hotel and there was a Chinese doorman. My brother had never seen a Chinese person. "Why do they have slanted eyes?" The only answer I could think of was that they were born that way. He accepted it.

Carriages were pulling over to the sidewalk of the hotel. The doorman tipped his hat and helped people to step down. I explained to my brother, "Those people are the rich people, and they must be living in the hotel."

Lucille and I continued walking. I was absorbed in my memories, and then I realized that we were on Plac Wolnosci. The first thing I wanted to see was the statue of Tadeusz Kosciuszko looking toward Piotrkowska Street. My eyes searched for more from the past, but all I saw was that the soul and glimmer of the city was gone. I was disillusioned. It was late, so we went back to the hotel.

The next morning, after breakfast at the hotel, we were ready to explore Lódz. I telephoned my driver to meet us outside the hotel within thirty minutes. As I turned around, an elderly gentleman came over and introduced himself to us. "My name is Jakub Bromberg, do you need a guide?" I thanked him, and started to walk away. Suddenly, I realized that he might be the only Jewish person in Lódz.

I turned around, "How much will you charge me?"

"Whatever you will give."

There wasn't any question in my mind that I wanted a Jewish person to be close to me. "Shalom Jakub, thank you for volunteering. I am sure you will be a great help."

The driver showed up and I told him where I wanted to go, but I wanted to direct him. He didn't object and we were on our way. First, I wanted to go to my home at 11go Listopada 58, where I had lived before the war. I directed him to Piotrkowska, to Plac Wolnosci and told him to make a left turn and take the first street on his left, but I asked him to drive slowly. He did as I instructed him. I looked at the street sign that said Ulica Stlingrada. I recognized the street immediately and started to point out many places from my past. Pointing to the street, I told Lucille, "Watch for number six and you will see a fire house. A little further up, there used to be a movie theater … and here … a bicycle racing track during the summer … and here … an ice-skating rink during the winter."

When we approached Ulica Cmentarna, I told the driver to park. We were standing across the street from where we had lived; my heart was rapidly beating—once more my doubts set in, "Why am I here?" I asked that no one speak to me. I looked up, saw 58—the three windows had closed draperies. I crossed the street and went through the gate toward the entrance of the stairs. I looked around. The brass banister was gone, some of the windows were broken and the same paint from 1939 was peeling away from the walls. The once shiny stairs were worn and dirty. After I reached the landing of the first set of stairs, I faced the two doors leading into our apartment. I felt brave, but my whole inside was crying. Our name was gone, and the bell and the red paint on the mahogany door were no longer there. For a minute I closed my eyes; when I opened them, would I see my mother or father at the door asking, "Where were you?" How often did I run up and down those stairs, two or three steps at a time, grabbing the bell and ringing it, only to be admonished for my behavior.

The driver and Jakub were standing next to me when I knocked at the door. There wasn't any answer. I knocked again and no one answered. The door on the left side opened up and a woman asked us what we wanted. Jakub explained to her that had I lived here before the war, and I wanted to show my wife the apartment. For a while there was silence. Then she apologized and told us that the people who were living in this apartment were on vacation. She invited us in. We talked for a while, thanked her for her hospitality and left. As we were walking down the stairs it dawned on me we should go up to the identical apartment on the floor above. We walked up and knocked on the door. A woman answered. After explaining to her why we were there, she invited us in. She asked us to sit down and she brought out cookies and tea. She was very gracious and charming. We talked for a while and I believed that she honestly sympathized with us. She showed us the improvements that had been done in her apartment. She didn't have a toilet and I guess if she had to use the toilet, she had to go down to the yard, or use the neighbor's. I spoke to both neighbors and each one went out of their way to be helpful.

During these conversations, one thing was haunting me. What if someone *had* opened the door of our apartment and invited us in? Would I have seen our furniture and the painting of Samson? Would I have seen some artifacts and have been able to touch them? All I could do was think … what if?

We went out to the yard, but this time I wasn't ten or eleven years old. I was seventy, a father and a grandfather. I looked around trying to visualize where my friends used to live. Pointing my finger at a window I told Lucille, "That is where Max Cliff used to live, and over there, Moishe Markowitz, and over there, Finkelstein, the shoemaker, who had two daughters."

There was no laughter of children. All the windows were dirty and shut. Back then, 119 families had lived here with maybe 100 children. I spent my childhood here from the age of three to the age of twelve. How sad the yard looked with the paint and the stucco coming off the walls of the building, exposing the raw bricks. I was thinking how poor these people were; I felt sorry for them.

Two men approached me and I started to converse with them. I explained to them that none of the people who had lived here were rich. They were shoemakers, carpenters, tailors and glaziers. Most of them had perished in the gas chambers, or were executed and put in a common grave somewhere. I felt their sympathy as one of the men raised his hand, pointing to the windows above. He said, "Look at our palace." He didn't mean to be funny.

We left; we had had enough for that day. I was emotionally drained. I discharged our guide and asked Jakub to join us for dinner. We spoke in Polish and Yiddish.

During dinner, Jakub told us about his life. "I fought with the Russians for the liberation of Lódz. My wife died a couple of years ago and I live on a small pension" (remember, he didn't solicit any money from us). "I have two children in Israel and both are serving in the army. In Lódz there are less than 500 Jews left, and half of those are really not Jews." I didn't say anything.

The next day I decided to take a ride to Kaminsk and visit my grandfather's grave. It took us less than two hours to get there. I knew what to expect. In 1939, in the first few days of the war, the town had been totally destroyed. My cousin, the first and oldest Shlomo Avigdor, had been killed. I remember how the families in Lódz mourned for this young twenty-one year old man. He was the first, but not the last, of our family to be a victim of the war. We arrived in Kaminsk and parked where the market used to be. Now, it was a beautiful square with a memorial statue in the center. I was looking for something of the past, and the only thing that was still standing was the church with its tall steeple. I decided for our own safety to go to the police station and state the purpose of my visit. I asked them where the Jewish cemetery was. They told me that a condominium had been built where it used to be. I decided that as long as I was there, I might as well see if I could obtain my birth certificate. Not only did I get mine, I also obtained my father's, including depositions from witnesses of our births. Jakub was a great help in obtaining some other documents. It seemed he knew everyone, and everyone knew him. We spent another hour looking around Kaminsk. No one had to tell me that there weren't any Jews living in this town anymore. We left and headed back to Lódz. I felt like spending the rest of the day just driving and walking through the streets.

We went down Ulica Zieromskiego to Poniatowskie Park, going past where my Uncle Moses had lived. We went where Poznanski's factories had been. The one-mile of buildings were vacant, and all the windows were broken. The chimneys that used to spew out all that smoke that sometimes made the city intolerable, as it was in the summer of 1938, were gone. Lódz was built around those textile factories and all of this had belonged to a Jewish family. As the factories went, so did the economy of Lódz.

The next day we went to what had been the ghetto, and again we went to the other home where I had spent a tragic five years. Rybna 17 was in much better shape than 11go Listopada 58. I went to the room where we had lived and a lock was hanging on the door. People started to ask me what I was doing there, and I explained that I had lived here. I asked who had the key. A man volunteered to ask the janitor for the keys. A woman came down, quite distressed. As she was putting the key in the lock I noticed her hands and body were shaking. This shaking was not from the cold, but from fear. I remembered those fears very well from my own past. I asked the driver whether she thought that I had come back to take the house away, and he agreed with me. I told him to tell her that I just wanted to see the room that we had lived in, that's all.

When she opened the door I noticed that the room had been converted to a coal bin. I walked in and once more my emotions took over. I looked at the room. There was a small window facing the same level as the surface of the yard. By this time, Lucille and the people gathering around us were wondering whether it was possible for five people to live here. I pointed out that we had managed to put in two narrow beds and a crib. We also had an iron stove; this was all we possessed in the ghetto. I turned around and saw two women, with tears in their eyes, making the sign of the cross the way Catholics often do.

I thanked the woman who had opened the door, and I shook her hand. We went into the yard and pointed out where the water well had been. That was where we hid the seventeen children who all perished. One of our "Boys" lived in the same building as I did. Moshe Pinchewski was a good friend of mine in the ghetto, and is a good friend today. He tells me stories about my family, which I had completely forgotten. Thank you Moshe.

Later, I went to the cemetery where my father was buried and found that there was a road and a row of trees over his grave—how sad it looked. Most of the gravestones had been vandalized, and the marble or brass plates stolen and used for decorations elsewhere.

The Polish guide was afraid to walk to the train station with us. I walked over there and a man motioned for Lucille to come over, too. The man was very polite, kissed Lucille's hand and we learned that he also lost family in the concentration camp. The station is a woodworking factory now. The next day, we went back to Warsaw. We arrived early in the day, and went back to the museum to obtain more documents from the archives.

On the rest of our trip we went to the home where Frederic Chopin was born, attended a concert at Poniatowski Palace, visited the famous Wieliczka salt mines and we were soaked by cold rain during a raft trip on the Dunajec River. We went to Zakopane, the mountain resort of Southern Poland, where I learned to ski. There we saw our first winter snow while going up in a cable car to the highest peak of the Tartars. When you spread your legs, your right leg is in Poland and your left leg is in Czechoslovakia.

All our tours ended October 1, and then we traveled to Riga, Latvia and arrived on October 3. The name of our hotel was "Latvia." When we arrived, there was a letter from a cousin who spends her summers in Riga, but we had missed her by three weeks.

We visited several interesting museums. One was part of the palace. The displays were old and dusty and just thrown together. It was disappointing. The art museums were better. The Latvian Ghetto Museum was very interesting. The American Latvian Ambassador was getting a tour through the museum while we were there. The Latvians had been treated very badly by the Russians. We took the Jewish tour of Riga. The Jews in Riga are very poor, and after paying for their necessities from their monthly pensions, nothing is left to live on. We visited the only Temple in Riga, where they have a soup kitchen open every day and spoke to the Rabbi about Lucille's family.

The pre-war synagogue, where 180 Jews were interred and burned alive with the help of the local Latvians, was next on our agenda; then a concentration camp that is now a memorial. The Russians put up several sculptures including a granite slab, and from within it there is the perpetual sound of a heartbeat, so those people who perished there will never be forgotten. The next place was the memorial park where Jews dug ditches, and 17,000 were executed and buried. Today, there are six mounds of dirt to commemorate their burial site, with grass and a Star of David placed in flowers.

We visited the only Jewish school, where uniformed guards stood at the front doors. The Lubavitcher movement runs the school. They are an organization located on Eastern Parkway, Brooklyn New York, near Brownsville, where Lucille had lived before we were married. We felt a certain pride to see a new generation of Jewish children being taught the alphabet. Rabbi Schneerson sent a young couple to oversee the work, and they are doing a good job. Most of the children are Russian. They spend the whole day in school and get all their meals there. Some had been circumcised at a later age. They all learn to speak three languages: Latvian, Russian and Hebrew.

We met a teacher who, although not familiar with Lucille's grandfather's family, provided us with some interesting information. When Lucille mentioned her cousin's family, who married in Riga, the teacher said her brother married into a Rusonik family, and she gave us her phone number in Israel. Lucille's cousin, who lived in Israel, could call to inquire if they were related. We intended to spend only three nights in Riga, and then go to Wilna, the capital of Lithuania. However, there was so much to see that we decided to stay there for the rest of our vacation, an additional 6 days.

We looked for Lucille's grandfather's apartment building and store and found them in good condition and operating. The building is one quarter of a block from the river. The river is very polluted because of commerce. Checking the archives at the Jewish Museum for Lucille's family history turned up nothing, because we forgot to use the names we received in Warsaw. Lifshitz is a common name in Riga. We met the chief Rabbi of Latvia, who said he remembered a family named Lifshitz. They lived in the building at #5 on the corner of Maskavas Street. The Rabbi gave us an address of a man who now lives in Israel, on a Kibbutz, and who is a friend of one of the Lifshitz's (Lipshitz) sons. Lucille's mother had always spelled her name with an F. The Rabbi said, "Lifshitz was spelled with an F, and my uncle spelled it with a P."

Our Latvian guide, a young woman, would not knock on an apartment door in Lucille's grandfather's building so we could see an apartment. She said, "There is a lot of crime in the area ... no one will let us go into the apartment." Lucille's grandfather had lived there a long time ago, and I didn't know which apartment had been his. In retrospect, I should have knocked anyway.

Most of the old cities in Eastern Europe are alike; Riga was not an exception. Right across the street from our hotel was a park, which led to the center of the Old Town. We marveled at the monuments, fountains, palaces and historic sites, which you only read about and see pictures of in history books. We are so bedazzled by our modern architecture in America, which sometimes is only twenty years old— but there, you are standing on sites built centuries ago. People were well dressed, stores were plentiful and restaurants and cafes were busy. It seemed the most popular thing to do, while people were walking and sitting around, was smoking and talking on a cellular phone. Latvia, like many of the Eastern European countries, is rebuilding. Approximately forty percent of Riga's population is Russian. The total Latvian population is approximately 3.5, and 1 million live in Riga. Three languages are spoken there: Latvian, Russian and German. We didn't have any problem communicating with the local people.

I am not sorry I went back to Poland. While there, I spoke to many students about the horror of the concentration camps. I saw their tears and their sorrow. I made sure that the people I spoke to knew I was a Zyd (Jew). When students in Krakow asked me why it took 52 years for me to come back, I told them about the episode at the train station, during my brief visit to Poland, before returning to Prague to leave for England. I also told them that Poles killed Jews *after* the war, and that 80 Jews died in the Kielce pogrom. I was not afraid to talk to anyone. Students and other Poles shook my hand, and looking at their faces, I knew that I had reached out to them. They understood my message and they reached out to me. The chip on my shoulder about Poland was no longer there.

I learned many things about the Poles during this time. As I continue to study the Holocaust, I learn more about things I could not have known back then. I used to be bitter and angry because I saw Poles who seemed to have had a better quality of life outside the ghetto fences and walls. I always wondered why no one threw over some bread or cheese or any kind of food to help. What I didn't know was, that if a Pole had done that, he or she and their entire family would have been executed. Would I have been any braver and risked my entire family if it had been the other way around? I didn't go to Poland to vent any hatred. I went to say goodbye. I returned home with a true sense of reconciliation.

It once was bright,
But now is tarnished and torn,
On our lapel,
That's where it was worn.
We wore it with pride,
We always will,
It's part of who we are,
A part the Germans could not kill.
I wore it when I was young,
I'll wear it when I am old.
If you look at the symbol,
A whole story can be told.
They took us away,
To a place called the ghetto,
A strange foreign place,
One we did not know.
No belongings of our own,
They took them all away
How could they treat us like this?
When we lived next door just yesterday.
The brightness began to fade,
As more and more began to die.
The edges began to tear,
more and more with every cry.

The Return To Lódz
A point for each,
Faith, love and loyalty.
One was for peace,
Two more for freedom and liberty.
The symbol showed our faith.
Liberation was never too far.
That's what we believed,
When we wore our Jewish Star.

*A Tribute to Victor Breitburg* by Cassi Matos, after Victor spoke to Mrs. Cohen Willard's 10H English class, at Amityville High School, in April, 2000.

# Chapter 22

## Teaching the Holocaust

I started speaking in 1954. I lived on Long Island where a new Holocaust Center had been established. They needed speakers and I was asked to speak at a school ... I never had spoken before, to adults or children. The teacher who had invited me was a Holocaust lecturer.

The first thing on my mind was not to get nervous. I sat down and said, "I am a Holocaust survivor. I was in concentration camps. What does that mean? It means losing your freedom. However, I lost more than my freedom. I found out that I lost my whole family." It was quiet. I said, "I counted you in your seats, in the same way children may have been counted and rounded up at the camps, and most of you would not have survived." I wanted to bring them to a place of understanding, not of being scared. I wanted them to sense what I suffered and saw. The teachers were crying as I walked among the students and talked to them. They understood what I was saying.

After that, I was invited to schools and temples. Speaking to them brought something out of me. I never cried, but I was able to talk to them in a way that they could understand. Many of these talks were reported in the local papers. My speaking schedule grew as a result of these articles.

An example of this was when a Rabbi was preparing for a trip, and was going to be short on time writing his weekly message. He phoned and asked me to speak at his temple. I lectured on the Kristellnacht. I shared how we had heard about it in Poland, and read about it in the papers. I tried to interpret those events in my own words as I had heard about those things, and how it affected me then. The teachers and the Rabbi came to shake my hand. They were crying. I just wanted them to know what prejudice of any kind can do. He gave me $500, and I respectfully told him that I didn't accept money for speaking. More came from the Sisterhood, so I informed them it would all be donated to the Holocaust Museum.

I had also given a talk to soldiers at Fort Hamilton, in Brooklyn, N.Y. I told them what General Eisenhower had said to General

Marshall after being at Ohrduf and Buchenwald, "I made the visit deliberately, in order to be in a position to give first hand evidence of these things if ever, in the future, there develops a tendency to charge these allegations merely to propaganda." The soldiers listened intently. Many of the soldiers knew about the Holocaust by this time.

I said, "There is never a winner in any war. The Holocaust was a tragedy for the whole world, not just the Jews. How many died on the battlefields, in the snow in Russia; how many died in the bombings during the war and to end the war? I believe that children are the biggest victims of war, and a dictator is always a dictator. I believe the Holocaust should be taught. Whoever says it never happened ... let them say so, I don't care!"

There are at least two ways to lecture: you can be strong and tough, or you can speak in a way that can manipulate the whole room to cry. Depending on the audience, I tone down some aspects of my lectures. The main thing to understand is, nothing can bring back anyone, yet we need to be aware of what prejudice can do. I didn't live through everything I speak about; I have studied beyond my own experiences. Often, a personal story gains more interest from an audience, however, my story is only an infinitesimal part of Holocaust history. I include more history than my own to give it a larger context and to stress that genocide is still a reality in many places of the world.

In my later years of teaching, well into my retirement, there are two years of lecturing in schools that were exceptional. The first was in 2000. The entire class was Afro-American students. I wondered how they would respond to my lecture. The teacher mentioned they had been studying Holocaust history. I began with our arrest, Auschwitz, the death of my family in the camps and the ghetto. It was mostly my story and the events in the camps like the hunger, the brutality and so on. After ninety minutes I finished and they all stood up. They were obviously very emotionally moved and came up to me. Before I left they all hugged me.

Sometime later, the teacher called me and asked me to return. She had an envelope for me. I thanked her and told her that I didn't take money for speaking.

"Oh no, this is much more precious than money."

# A Rage To Live

When I entered the classroom, all the students stood up, and I was given a large manila envelope. It was pages of poems written by Mrs. Cohen-Willard's students, reflecting on what I had shared with them. This handwritten note was included:

*Dear Mr. Breitburg,*

*My classmates and I thoroughly enjoyed your presentation and wanted to present you with thank you letters and poems to reflect how moving your words were to us. We hope you will enjoy reading these as much as we enjoyed hearing your presentation.*

*Sincerely,*

*From all of us in Mrs. Cohen-Willard's English class*

A letter from a student was also very meaningful:

*Dear Mr. Breitburg,*

*I highly appreciate the speech you gave my classmates and I. It meant so much to me, because now I can pass the stories of the men and women who suffered during the Holocaust. Now I know that I can tell people about your story and hope that the story will never die. I never really thought of the Holocaust as I did when you told your story. I have never heard a survivor, or a witness, speak in person. I thought that it was a very kind and brave thing you did to speak to us. And your story really touched me. I thought it was very nice when you talked about how you decided to jump off that wagon that immediately brought the other passengers to death. And when you were in Auschwitz, you were deciding between either going with the mothers and children or with the men, and instead, you were shoved to the side that would live. I think that that is an amazing thing. I think that those signs tell you that you definitely have a purpose in life. I think that your purpose in life was to keep the story of all the men and women who died, living. It wasn't just fate or destiny that made you live through that, it was courage. I know you told us that at one point you didn't care whether you lived or died, but I know there was at least a little bit of courage inside of you when you didn't have hope. I don't think that words can describe the tragedy that you had to go through. I don't know how it must have been but I think that you are an extremely strong man now because of it. My grandfather was a Prisoner of War in WWI. He had to also go through an extremely long and strenuous walk, in the snow. So when you said that you had to walk in those conditions and everything like that, I immediately thought of my grandfather, and I think that was what touched me the most. Having a relative go through that is a horrible thing, that was when I knew why you didn't exactly want to tell your children. I understand, because when my grandfather told me about his war stories, I was crying. I think it was better that you didn't tell them until later, because I know how it feels to be the relative. I think that your courage and strength and will to live, makes you a great person. I want to thank you, again, for the wonderful, and very touching speech you gave and I want to let you know that your story will always be alive in my family.*

*Sincerely, Meghan E. Tello*

After that, I spoke to them each year before they graduated. They were a wonderful and unusual class. How much discrimination did *they* endure? Their poetry expresses much emotion and perception. I did meet some students, years later, in restaurants and other places, and I told them I was very proud of them. I continued to further my own studies of the Holocaust to see the bigger picture.

How do we stop bullies, perhaps the next Hitler? How do you talk to a young kid and explain that there was no family left? I never wanted my talks just to be a bunch of sob stories. I wanted them to relate to the difficulties in their own lives because of their ethnic backgrounds. We should talk more about all the discrimination in the world, not just the Holocaust.

Before and after this, I was also speaking at a number of Temples. I received a very kind letter:

*April 9, 1999*

*Dear Victor,*

*On behalf of the Hewlett-East Rockaway Jewish Centre, and myself, I want to thank you so much for coming to speak to the Congregation on the Eighth Day of Pesach, April 8, 1999, about your family, and what life was like for you in Lódz at the time of the Holocaust.*

*To say your talk was "moving" is an understatement. I know that everyone felt like they were almost there in that town with you. I know for me, it hit a nerve. Your statement that you feel "guilt" for surviving has been my battle for years. I have mostly overcome my "guilt feelings" by being "a mitzva person". I'm ready, willing and able to help out anyone that needs it. And, in addition, I'm on the religious side, and that has helped too. But the feelings of wonder and "why me" will always be my "peckle." I know one thing, luck, courage and faith had a lot to do with surviving.*

*I hope you know that you stirred many thoughts in people's heads about the Holocaust that brought them out of their world of complacency. Everyone feels so comfortable all the time that it is almost unreal to hear someone like you talk about survival. Victor, "thank you, thank you," again for being with us and sharing your life.*

*The enclosed is the Synagogue's donation to the Suburban Temple. I wish it could have been more. I hope that Suburban Temple is able to get a new Torah. If ever you need any help with this project please let me know.*

# Teaching the Holocaust

*All good wishes to you and your family; I hope you have lots of naches from them and continue doing all the good things that you are doing for others.*

*Affectionately,*

*Marion Hauser*

Another truly significant teaching time came at the end of my formal speaking days, just before we moved to Florida in 2005. Regina White, the Educational Director of the Holocaust and Education Center of Nassau County, asked me to do her a favor. She wanted me to lecture about the Holocaust at the Amityville High School. The Principal had requested that I speak to the 2005 senior class. I felt awkward lecturing there. I had already spoken there twice, and this class had about ninety students. Ninety percent of the class was Afro–American, and the rest were a multi-ethnic mixture.

They rung the bell, the Principal introduced me to the students as a Holocaust survivor, handed the microphone to me and commented, "The class of 2005 is all yours." I had two hours to help them understand the tragedy of the Holocaust, and to prepare them to withstand the Holocaust deniers, who in the future, might try to convince them that it had never happened. I wondered if they would be strong enough to stand up to those kinds of people, and if my lecturing would help to make a difference in how they might think. I slowly started, while trying to make eye contact with every student.

"Listen to me … nothing can be done to reverse what happened to me, and at the same time I don't ever want it to happen to anyone else. I will take you through the journeys, the starvation, the pain of seeing your friends dieing and through the gas chamber crematoriums." There was silence in the room. All eyes were riveted on me, and many girls were crying. I didn't want to hurt them, but I wanted them to know that there can be a very short distance from discrimination and ethnic hatred, to a genocide or Holocaust.

The class bell rung, and nobody was moving. I looked around the room, and I noticed that there were also many teachers with us now. The principal nodded that I should go on with my lecture. When I finished, I stopped and asked if there were any questions … they were slow in coming, but I was used to that. Students can be very sensitive and are usually afraid to ask certain questions because they think they might hurt me. The one question I truly hoped to be asked came, with these words, "What are the differences between slavery and the Holocaust?"

After a few moments I responded, "I will not trivialize the loss of the slaves who had perished on the routes to the Americas. I will not trivialize the loss of the slaves by their master's cruelty and horrible treatment. I will not trivialize the loss of the slaves and the demise of their families. I will not trivialize the losses, because the true figures will never be known. I have studied your history from Booker T. Washington to Jessie Jackson. I have studied about the African Kingdoms. I have learned about the university of Timbuktu and the great wealth of Africa. I have learned how the European nations raped the wealth out of Africa, and that the slaves were bought for work to make plantation owners wealthier—making the slaves nothing more than a commodity. The Jew was sent to the ghettos and the concentration camps for extinction."

I finished my lecture. It was very quiet, but slowly students started to drift over toward me. Girls hugged me and boys shook my hand. After all the students left, the faculty and the principal came over with a question, "How were you able to speak to the class for ninety minutes without losing a single student's attention?" I asked the other teachers why they had come to hear my lectures. A Jewish woman answered, "Why do I go to the synagogue every year on Yom Kippur?"

I was invited to join the faculty for lunch, but I had to decline because I had an appointment with my lawyer. We had recently sold our house, and after the closing, we were leaving for Maryland to visit my daughter Denise. From there, we were off to Florida to begin the next stage of our lives at Wynmoor. I walked outside; the weather was crispy and cold, and as I looked at the bare trees I said, "Yes, winter has arrived. Wednesday I will be in Florida."

# Chapter 23

## A Final Adjustment

As soon as we had moved to Wynmoor, we were involved in all kinds of activities, programs and classes, including writing. Socializing with old and new friends became a way of life, and I was very involved in the Democratic Party organization. After awhile, the family began to notice that Lucille was slowing down and was not as energetic and vibrant as we were all used to seeing her. Lucille became ill in 2009. She had liver and pancreatic cancer. She died three weeks after being diagnosed, on August 6. Her last words to me were, "Victor you gave me everything I could have wanted."

My daughters remembered their mother in this way:

> *Our mother had a hard beginning, She lost her mother when she was only 9 and was left as the protector of her mentally retarded sister, Rose. Maybe because of this, it was hard for her to understand that part of growing up is separating from your parents. She told me once that she always dreamed about what it would have been like to have a mother growing up. She loved her mother's aunts and uncles and their kids who were her cousins. We visited them in the Bronx, in Peekskill, and at Beach. My father's relatives were also an important part of her life and became her family too- especially Shirley, who traveled down from NY to be here and see my mother, and her sister and parents.*
>
> *Lucille fiercely protected her kids and always tried to help them and everyone around her. She was president of our high school PTA-much to my dismay because of the bad-girl image I cultivated in those days-, she volunteered at Holly Patterson nursing home, she worked with the League of Women Voters, and she helped at a homeless shelter. Her love for flowers and plants drew her to the Levittown Garden Club where she met many close friends. Lucille joined the local chapter of the Cooperative Extension where she made the many arts and*

*crafts that decorate her home. She wrote letters and clipped newspaper articles she thought would interest us. She never ate until the rest of us were served, and she never spent money on herself for clothes or treats.*

*I think my mother and father rescued each other from the hard times they went through growing up. They met at night school in Brooklyn. They walked home together to Brownsville where they both lived and found out that they had much in common, including losing their parents when they were young. They found stability in each other. She was making almost twice as much money, an amazing $75.00 a week compared to my father's $45.00. She was the secretary for the Director of Employment for New York State and helped the Boys Club of Brownsville get built, and was a leader in the local Y.*

*After 3 years of dating my father proposed. They planned and paid for their own wedding on June 11, 1949, and the smiles on the wedding pictures show their love. My mother had a great smile. They were married for 60 years this June and were rarely apart through that whole time. Even in the end, my father slept by her side and held her hand at the Hospice Center. He built a good home for them; some of it with his own hands, and they built a life together. I don't think either could have imagined how it would be when they first met.*

*Our mother was a walker with strong legs. She wasn't an outdoors person-she was a Brooklyn girl who didn't see why people make a big deal about the redwoods-but she walked everywhere to take care of us and to make our life better. I remember her walking home from the grocery store pulling a heavy basket of the family's weekly food. I remember her walking to my elementary school so she could then walk me to dance classes and home again. She walked us to doctor's appointments, she walked the dog, her Brandy, and she walked to the bus stop. She walked the streets of Europe with my father, around the pyramids in Egypt, and the halls of museums. Never fast, never lightly, but walking on and on. It was especially hard to see her legs fail her in her later years.*

# A Rage To Live

*Lucille had a high school education, and always wanted to learn more. She started taking college classes in her 70's and even did her homework for her grammar class. She chose Elder-hostels for vacations -not for their comfortable settings, but to learn. She took up knitting with a vengeance and loved learning new crafts. She loved plays and music and museums.*

*She was so proud of her grandchildren. We always heard about the proud stories she told others about their achievements and how well they were doing. She was so worried about them when they were born -especially Maya because she was the first. But as she added grandkids and made new friends, she kept up with people she shared her life with, including friends who she met as a small child-some before she was old enough to go to school.*

*My mother also had a strong sense of right and wrong. It was important to her that other people respected her decisions. She wasn't religious, but had a strong moral core. But she was also a woman who was afraid of many things and of what others thought -maybe because she didn't have the security of parents' love growing up. Strangely, she said that dying wasn't one of those fears, although suffering in the end was. I hope she didn't suffer too much -it was very hard watching her the last few days as she struggled to breathe.*

*We're so grateful that my parents made wonderful new friends and were able to be near old friends as well once they moved to Wynmoor. My mother loved the nature club and shows, and even though she rarely wrote, she loved listening to what others had written in the writers club. We really appreciate you all for being here and for the loving support you've given my parents.*

*Lucille—we love you, and will miss you.*

# Epilogue

*Reflections*

I have lived a prosperous and happy life. I had a wonderful marriage with Lucille. My older daughter Denise is a Senior Scientist at the Smithsonian Environmental Research Center. Her husband, Mark, is an administrator with the St. Mary's County Public School System. He is the Coordinator of Special Programs. Their daughter, Maya, is in the MS program in Environmental Management at Yale and their son, Eli, has a B.A. from Goucher College in Anthropology and is determining a career path. My younger daughter, Myra, is an Assistant Professor at Farmingdale University of New York.

# Epilogue

In this later season of my life I have a companion, Ruth, with whom I share so many interests. We love to write, her specialty is poetry. We enjoy concerts and the opera and films, but playing bridge is her domain. She keeps me in line with practical things I sometimes don't like to be bothered with. Ruth's husband Buddy, died before Lucille. The four of us had been friends for many years.

The events of my life are only unique because of some of the circumstances, which for any of us, makes the differences in our lives. I have been able to do what many survivors of the Holocaust have done … go on, live a normal life and accomplish something along the way. I am not special for having done that. Many of "The Boys" became successful in business, like Ben Helfgott, who was also an Olympian weightlifter for England. Some went on to become rabbis, teachers and professors. This week, right here in Broward County, a ninety year-old man just completed a college degree.

What has been the most difficult part of reconciling the events of my life, to my present well being, were my thoughts after I had returned from my 1996 visit to Poland; having seen the places where I had lived and those places that had become a part of my life during the Holocaust. During those life-altering times, I had never had a chance to say goodbye—to anyone.

While visiting Birkenau, I stood at the spot where the railroad widens, facing the barracks and the crematoriums. I saw my mother, my brother and my sister on that fateful day of August 15, 1944. I said goodbye, and asked them for forgiveness. I went to my father's grave in Lódz, now under the pavement, and said goodbye. I went back to Kaminsk—I couldn't find the grave of my grandfather, and said goodbye. And finally, standing at the grave of my grandmother here in the United States, I asked for forgiveness for not being able to save her children and her grandchildren. I realize it was not within my ability to do it, but nevertheless, the guilt is there. During those very trying years, I was afraid, but I had a rage to live. If I had died, then Hitler would have succeeded.

# The Extras – 1: Victor and Me

Often, the first question I am asked about working on the book, depending on where I am and who I am with is, "Are you Jewish?"

The second question is, "How did a Baptist pastor make this connection?"

It all began in 2009 while I was putting down some ideas for a play about a Holocaust survivor. I had been doing some research on my Polish background and I was looking to do some writing other than my theological work, just for the exercise.

During my research, I found some of Victor's articles at the JewishGen website and with copyright necessities in mind, I wrote to Roni Seibel Liebowitz to make an inquiry.

*From: Roni S. Liebowitz*

*Subject: RE: LARG Inquiry*

*Date: November 10, 2009 4:30:19 PM EST*

*To: Joseph Krygier*

*Hi Joseph,*

*Your research and forthcoming play are exciting.*

*I just spoke with Victor Breitburg, and he would be happy to hear from you.*

*I forwarded your e-mail to him so he will know what it's about when you make contact.*

*Good luck with your project. Please let me know how it progresses.*

*Regards,*

*Roni*

*From: Joseph Krygier*

*Subject:      thank for your life story*

*Date:         September 11, 2009 9:29:11 AM EDT*

*To: Victor Breitburg*

*Dear Mr. Breitburg,*

*I was very blessed to read the accounts of your life story in Lódz and the camps and your eventual life in America.*

*It was particularly interesting to me because for some time now I have been doing some specific research on Lódz and those who survived the ghetto and the camps.*

*I have had an idea to write a one-act play, about 80-90 minutes in length, for a while now. The main character survived Lódz and the ghetto.*

*The story line of his life that I was concocting turns out to be similar to your story and your story helps me with many details that I have been looking for to make the play accurate.*

*The title of the play is "Chagrined".*

*One theme in the play is the use of humor during the Holocaust with a focus on how it was used by those in the ghettos, and in the camps as a survival mechanism.*

*I know for many, perhaps this was not the case, but my research has shown that for others it was. I have been reading Professor Chaya Ostrower's doctoral extract on the subject and other sources.*

*My point in sharing this with you is this-would you allow me to use your story as a basis for my character? Of course if it were ever published and performed, you would be credited as the source for the character etc.*

*I have a friend from my acting days, Lee Wilkof, who is a well-known actor in film, television and on Broadway. In the Auschwitz film, "The Grey Zone", he played the Jewish man who refused to give his watch to the SS officer. His performance was heartbreaking. If/when finished and if good enough to be produced, especially in New York, my hope is that Lee might be willing, able and available, to do the play someday.*

*A personal note: My father's parents were Polish. They were born in Buffalo. Grandmother was a Batkowski. My grandfather was a Krygier (I thought it was a German name spelled in a Polish spelling. But it is a Polish and Jewish variant of Kryger. My family did not keep very good records of their heritage. I am not sure from what part of Poland or Germany my great grandparents came from. I am still working on it. I have been to Poland 6 times. The part of Poland my great-grand parents lived in was at one time considered West Prussia. They considered themselves German-Poles. It has been difficult to confirm this, and it seems that there may be more Jewish families with the present spelling of the name than there are those of Polish heritage. I don't know why the spelling was changed.*

*I realize this is quite a request and would understand if you would not be interested.*

*It would be my privilege to try and accomplish this project with your co-operation.*

*I live in Buffalo, N.Y. If it were possible, I could even come to meet with you sometime.*

*I pastor a small Baptist Church part time, and I own a small business providing training seminars for the NYSDEC.*

*Sincerely,*

*Joseph Krygier*

We began talking to each other once a week, and in November I suggested that we have a face to face in Coconut Creek. I made the arrangements for a flight in February 2010. When I confirmed my flight with Victor he said, "Your room is ready for you."

As I walked down the arrival ramp at the Fort Lauderdale Airport, I immediately recognized Victor; we met and shook hands. He asked, "How was your trip Reverend?" I smiled and told him it went well. The first thing we did was to go to dinner. Even when I have arrived late in the evening during subsequent visits, the first question Victor usually asks is, "Are you hungry?" As Victor says, "If you want to live, you have to eat." The second thing he would say at the airport is, "Now we have to find my car." Parking can sometimes be a bit complex at this airport because of the ongoing construction in the parking ramp. Each time I have visited, it has been a different experience. Once, we rode around the ramp four times in an open shuttle trying to find the car. We laughed a lot. As Victor says, "If you want to live, you have to laugh." We can say that we are alive and well.

The first thing I noticed when I walked into Victor's home, was symmetry in the way the oversized furniture was laid out. There was a large dining table with six chairs and one large sofa with three sections in a partially curved arrangement. There was a waist high cabinet separating the two areas with family pictures on the top. Along the wall to my right were pictures of his granddaughter Maya, during her Peace Corp service in Africa. A large, framed print of Sandra Bierman's *The Blue Cat* was the next thing on the wall. Then I noticed a glass cabinet with various styles and types of ceramic pieces. Next to that was a longer cabinet with pictures and some smaller sculpture pieces that included Native American and Cowboy art. There was also an iPod player on the cabinet. On the opposite wall, there were large posters and other art prints, some with Jewish themes.

His enclosed patio, which overlooks the golf course, had been converted to an office and there were various awards and certificates of appreciation on the wall above his computer. There was a small modernistic sculpture on the other side of the room on a wall shelf, and a fantastic four-panel cartoon caricature of Victor—bowling.

I was then escorted to my room, which is where Victor has his library, music and many photo albums and scrapbooks in the closet. I knew I had a vast amount of source material to look through once we started working. At another time, when it was necessary, he showed me more in his bedroom.

Victor gave me free reign of his home. Closets, cabinets, boxes of stored materials of his writing, newspaper articles, '45 Aid society Journals and other awards that were not on display. If he had to keep an appointment, I would often go with him or I would stay and work and could go out as I pleased for a walk or to the gym or for a swim.

By the end of our first week together, he said, "Joe, I can't call you Reverend while we are together in my house like this. We are too close now, but I will still call you that in public. It reminded me of the first conversation we had by phone in September.

"How should I call you, Minister, Reverend, Pastor or what?"

"Joe is fine."

"O.K. Reverend."

I knew that we were going to have an interesting relationship.

The many hours of talking, doing video interviews, reading articles and newspaper clippings inevitably leads to planning some time away from the work. Lunch and dinner, exercise in the pool or the gym, running some errands and shopping were the ways we normally took a break during the day. In the evenings we might go to a concert at the beautiful Fine Arts Center at Wynmoor or go to a music night presentation/seminar. The one we attended was part one of a filmed version of the opera *Boris Gudanov*. We also attended a cross-cultural meeting at the town community center and participated in a lecture and talk session with the cultural representative of the Seminole Nation for that part of Florida. It was a fascinating evening.

And there were the evenings we just went back to work for an hour or two.

The Wednesday of my first week with Victor, we had put in a long day. We went to dinner a little earlier and when we came back, Victor wanted to spend some more time talking about a particular topic concerning the time he had spent in Scotland. We decided we would stay up a little later that evening, and that he would take a nap, until about 8 P.M. This was at about 6:30 P.M.

I was doing some writing, and by 8 P.M. it seemed quiet in Victor's room, so I retired to my room to catch up on the news via CNN, and then I was going to watch a movie. About fifteen minutes later Victor said, "OK Joe, time for breakfast, let's go."

As I started to walk to the living room, I said, "Victor, you really feel like breakfast?" I came out of the room and there he was: shaved, showered, hair combed, in a different shirt, shorts, sneakers, and ready to go.

"Yes, come on let's go. I had a good night's sleep and I know you want to get a lot done today."

As he started walking towards the door I said, "But Victor, it's 8:30 in the evening."

"What?"

I wasn't sure if he had heard me or if he was just surprised. He hadn't heard me. He had been having some problems with his hearing aid.

"Victor ... it's 8:30 ... Wednesday night."

He stopped, turned around, looked at me and we just starting laughing so hard that it hurt.

He had set his alarm clock for 8 P.M. He had been so tired and had slept so soundly for that hour and a half, that when he woke up, he thought it was the next day. He had to call Ruth and let her know, laughing through most of the conversation. After that we spent some time talking before deciding at 10:30 P.M. to call it a day. Even weeks later, he shared that story with my wife Deborah over the phone, and we still laugh about it.

The next morning, before breakfast, we had a workout in the pool. Most of the time we had breakfast at the Bagel Hut or the 19th Hole and occasionally, we would eat in. When we got back, this happened a few times during the course of my six visits, someone needed Victor to respond to a need or a question about the condo. My wife can testify to that. It happened when she was with me on my second visit. He served as an officer for their section of units. These were always opportunities for me to meet other people and even to spend some time getting to know them. I worked the rest of the morning making notes until Victor came back.

We worked together for a while and then we went to the 19th Hole for lunch. I met so many people there during my visits. On this occasion there were some Jewish ladies sitting at the adjacent table. He introduced me to them and said, "This is my friend, the Reverend. He knows the Almighty. If you shake his hand you will be converted and go to heaven." We could not escape the ensuing laughter.

That evening, Victor, Ruth, and I had dinner at Victor's with another friend. Her husband had been with Victor from Auschwitz to America and had passed away a number of years ago. Ruth, and her husband of sixty years, Buddy, who had died a few years ago, had known Victor and Lucille for over 25 years. Ruth was born in America. She had been a model (photography) and a primary school teacher. Buddy was involved with major productions of live television in New York since the fifties and other areas of production. Our other guest was also a Holocaust survivor.

She was having problems with feeling bitter towards some family members. After dinner Victor said, "You don't listen to your friends who want to help you, you don't talk with your Rabbi, so now you are going to talk to my friend Joe, the Reverend; she did. I gave her the best counsel I could from Proverbs and kept the teaching in light of the Torah, as I understood it. She said it helped and that she would try to obey God.

Victor was pleased and he said, "But Joe can't *convert* me, because I am already circumcised."

Yes, we all started laughing. "Who's trying?" I said, laughing even more. "But Victor, I am circumcised too. You are outwardly circumcised and as you desire the Almighty in your life you work to please him by external obedience to Torah. I have a circumcised heart by the Almighty's grace and my obedience, out of love for Him, flows from the inside out toward Him, and it causes me to love the Word of God."

He looked at me, pointed his finger, cracked a smile and with a laugh said, "Oh you are a wise one." We all laughed, hilariously.

On the last day of my first visit, Friday, Victor shared with me that he wanted to write more than just the articles that had been published at the JewishGen website and in some journals and newspapers. He wanted to put his writing in some kind of a simple book format for his family. I encouraged him to do it, gave him some suggestions and subsequently he asked me to edit and to co-author the book. Considering that I was only there to work out the details of writing a play a based on Victors life, it is amazing how fast the project grew.

My job has been to help arrange his autobiographical articles and sketches in the most meaningful order of telling his story. Rewrite, as necessary, for clarity, better choice of words and so on. I have also added objective historical data that coincides with his personal narrative to give the events of his life a broader historical context, as it parallels the events of the Holocaust and its aftermath.

We have also produced a series of non-scripted and non-rehearsed, informal interviews and segments of Victor reading from his articles which, once the book is published, will be posted at www.tolifeink.com and at JewishGen Shetlinks.

Between my first two visits, one year after Lucille had died, Victor invited me to the Matzevah (unveiling of the headstone and the placing of a remembrance stone instead of flowers), in remembrance of Lucille. It was a very special invitation. Sadly, I could not attend due to a conflict with my job.

My wife, Deborah, accompanied me on my second trip. We could write pages about the talks Victor, Ruth, Deborah and I had and the ones where she and Victor went one on one. And again, once all was said and done, in agreement or disagreement, you could not escape the laughter.

During this visit, Paul Gast came up from Miami to spend time with us. I had talked to Paul during my first trip by phone. Victor wanted to introduce him to me. We recorded about two hours of conversations with Paul and Victor, comparing notes and looking through some of the '45 Aid Society Journals. Paul and Victor both grew up in Lòdz, but never knew each other until they were liberated and resettled in England, at Windemere. Martin Gilbert mentions Paul in his book, *The Boys,* and so does Joseph J. Preil in *Holocaust Testimonies: European Survivors and American Liberators in New Jersey*.

Paul is an accomplished lecturer in the mandated Holocaust Studies programs in the Miami area and hosts trips to Poland as well. He and his daughter are very active in forming chapters of the Second Generation, those who are the descendants of "The Boys" and the original '45 Aid Society. I had opportunities to meet with Paul, and meet his wife, during three of my six trips to Fort Lauderdale, including one visit to his home. I did a separate thirty-minute interview with Paul about his perspective on teaching the Holocaust.

Paul shared that he had been reticent about sharing his personal experiences concerning the Holocaust for many years. But once he retired, he had a change of mind. When he teaches, he shares a brief background about the loss of his parents. He was an only child, and out of the rest of his extended family of eighteen to twenty people, he was the only Polish survivor of the Holocaust. He had four family members who survived in Germany. His journey began in the Lòdz Ghetto, then moved to Auschwitz, Ravensbrück and finally to Ludwigslust, and liberation in 1945. Ravensbrück was also the camp where Corrie Ten Boom's family was incarcerated, as told in *The Hiding Place*. Corrie ten Boom received recognition

175

from the Yad Vashem Remembrance Authority as one of the "Righteous Among the Nations." In 1952, Paul was drafted into the Army, and served in Korea. He was an accountant and a company manager during his business career. One thing he stresses in his teaching about the Holocaust is that it is not just something that occurred many years ago. The fact that this lesson from history is sometimes met with apathy and seems not to be universally understood for the horrible thing that it was, is why he emphasizes the need to recognize that Genocide has existed and continues to exist in our contemporary world in Darfur, Sudan, Somalia and other places. His concern is to try to have students understand the necessity for religious and ethnic tolerance with the hope of preventing these kinds of tragedies.

During my third trip, I talked with a dear lady during lunch, for a quite a while. Being a pastor, and Victor always introduces me that way, leads to some inevitable questions about the why's and how's of becoming a minister. We shared things about ourselves and found we both loved the art of dance. At her later age, she was very fit and still teaching a dance class. She invited me to attend, but with my flight schedules I would always miss the opportunity. Toward the end of our conversation, she shared with me that she did not believe in God. Whenever she saw me, either walking down the road, while she was driving her golf cart, during an afternoon break on my way to the gym, or at the restaurant, she would always wave or say hello.

The next time I saw her at lunch, I walked up to her and she said, "You probably don't like me anymore."

"Why?"

"I told you I don't believe in God."

"Why should that influence whether or not I like you. I do like you and look forward to seeing you when I am visiting here. For one thing, you have such a pleasant smile." We gave each other a little hug and I hope to see her on my next visit.

And then there is the time one of the groundskeepers, they do an excellent job of maintaining the complex, said, "Victor, aren't you going to introduce me to your son. I see you with him all the time but you have never introduced us."

"Oh, this isn't my son—this is my friend Joe. He is a minister. He is helping me to write my book. However, we are considering adoption."

Well, by now I think you can get a good idea of what the weeks we spent together were like. Only God's providence could have brought me to this place in my life.

I have met the condo managers, workers, some residents, favorite waitresses, Victor's bowling team, his GP, heart doctor and physical therapist. On my third visit, his cousin and his wife were visiting from New York and along with Paul, his wife Edith and Ruth, we went out to dinner and had a wonderful time.

One day during a swimming break, Victor was talking to one of the ladies exercising in the pool, and I heard in a clear and loud voice, "Victor, you're going to be famous."

Victor and I have discussed politics, social issues, the President, labor, education, history, music, theater, the history of television, the Bible, interfaith issues—you name it, and Ruth at times has been part of those conversations. And in the end there has always been an increased appreciation of one another regardless of differing opinions, and laughter. One thing that is very important to Victor, and has been for many years, is the future for children, all over the world. This is a passionate concern. Education issues, prejudice, political instability, the threats of war, disease, famine, no jobs and so on are issues that we talked about in various contexts, almost every day.

Thank you Dorothy, Gert, Mary, Judy, Jack, Rudy and so many more for talking with me while I was hanging around Wynmoor. Thank you for sharing something about your life with me.

During these past two years I have come to know and love Victor as a friend. I could write much more about our times together, and for one who has lived through what Victor has, we could have added so much more. Just going through Victor's photographs and newspaper articles reveals the possibility of a much larger book. I hope I have shaped the story of Victor's life into this volume in a meaningful way. We were not attempting to write the equivalent of a presidential memoir or the biography of a famous general or author. As I wrote in the introduction, if anything comes as a result of this book, perhaps more Genocide survivors will be encouraged to share their stories, for each is of value. And I hope my play, *Chagrined,* will find an audience and might be able to be used as a living history lesson in school assemblies and other kinds of special gatherings.

My last conversation with Victor at the end of my first visit, while stepping out of the car at the airport to leave for Buffalo, set the tone for the next two years of our relationship.

"Victor, I will do my best to help you tell your story in a way that will be meaningful for your family and anyone else who may read this book."

"Joe, I know it will be a lot of work for you. Maybe we will make a few bucks together. But no matter what, we are friends for life.

**Victor, Ruth, Deborah and Joe**

**Joe, Paul and Victor comparing notes from '45 Aid Society Journal**

# A Rage To Live
## Farewell and Shalom My Friend

Victor and I continued our close friendship after the publication of our book. On the one-year anniversary of the publication of our book, in April 2013 I published a gift hardcover copy and brought it with me for our visit with him in Florida. Deborah was with me.

I did a series of interviews with him reflecting on our friendship and the book.

In October 2013, Myra let me know that they had moved Victor to Long Island to be placed in a Residential facility for people with dementia.

In November 2014 we visited Victor at the Gerwyn Home on Long Island with his daughter Myra and Roni Seibel Liebowitz and her husband. It was a wonderful day with some laughter and Victor periodically forgetting my name. The stories are too many to share here.

Victor had a fulltime personal aid. His name was Mohammed, a wonderful, caring soul. The family loved him for the care he gave to Victor. I met him and talked with him frequently by phone when I would call Victor. During one call Victor said," I want to touch you."

By April of 2015, Victor was transferred to Harbor House on Long Island. Alzheimer's was the culprit that led to that move.

We visited him at that time and again on November 13, 2015, the day Paris was attacked by Islamic Terrorists.

Soon after that Victor lost all recognition of family and friends.

Again, the Lord provided a wonderful caring person, a girl named Ronie to be Victor's aid during the Corona outbreak.

She was offered the opportunity to go home on leave to be with her children. She said she would stay with Victor.

He did not die from Corona, but in his last days Ronie was the only one who could be with him.

I participated in the Zoom funeral service with some family and friends.

## OBITUARY

Victor Shlomo Breitburg
MAY 8, 1927 – MAY 29, 2020
Victor Shlomo Breitburg was born on May 8, 1927 in Kaminsk, Mazovia, Poland and passed away on May 29, 2020 in Oyster Bay, New York and is under the care of Star of David Memorial Gardens Cemetery and Funeral Chapel.

Committal Service will be held on June 3, 2020 at 11:45 am at Star of David Memorial Gardens Cemetery in the Garden of Aaron II, 7701 Bailey Road, North Lauderdale, FL.

# The Extras – 2: The Old Man and His Shadow
## by Victor Breitburg with Joseph G. Krygier

"Madelyn please come in!"

"I am here," I heard her whisper.

I looked around toward where the voice was coming from. "Aha, there you are."

All I could see without my glasses was her silhouette.

"May I have my glasses please?"

"Here are your glasses Mr. Fried."

As she came closer I saw a faint smile on her face. She was a middle-aged widow, polite and helpful. She bathed me every day, dressed me, cooked and made sure that I had clean clothes to wear.

"Mr. Fried, you had a fever last night. How do you feel this morning?"

"How do you expect me to be?" Why am I so grouchy to her; she is so devoted to me. "Damn, I asked you to call me Jim."

"Did you sleep here?" I did not answer right away.

"Yes. Madelyn please dress me, I want to go to the park."

"Are you all right? Last night you had a fever, and you refused to eat. If you want to go to the park you will have to eat and take your medicine first."

"OK."

She gave me my medicine and some soup. I ate a little bit, for her sake; it was very difficult and painful for me to swallow.

Slowly, she dressed and shaved me. "If we are going to go out I have to dress you properly," Madelyn said.

After she finished, I felt like my whole body was on fire, but it was the Fourth of July with The Symphony playing. She handed me my cane and was supporting me under my other arm. As we entered the park, I noticed my favorite bench was still empty.

"Madelyn, there is my bench. I have to rest a little while … from there I will be able to hear the music. What time is it?"

"It is three o'clock Mr. Fried."

"It's Jim, damn it!"

I should have known that when the shadow is in front, and getting larger, it must be at least three o'clock.

"Jim, who are you talking to? "Madelyn asked"

"To my shadow, it started before you were born. Do you want me to tell you about it?" She nodded yes.

"My romance with the shadow started when I was about four years old. My parents were holding my hand when I noticed two tall images and one small one walking ahead of us. Who is walking in front of us?"

"Go and find out," my father said.

The image was coming out from my shoes, and when I tried to touch it, it changed. I stood up and started to turn. Wherever I turned there was a different image.

"Mommy, what is that" I asked?

"Well, we call it a shadow, and every one of us has their own. You can dance and change it if you want to," my mother said with a laugh.

"Time passed, and the shadows of our family grew by two; a brother and a sister. We had our shadows, and the birds were clapping their wings and dogs were barking to our delight. Our walls, ceilings and floors became our projection screens. We tried to catch each other's shadows to no avail."

"It was a happy time. But, the dark clouds obscured our family. First, the shadow of my father vanished, next my mother's, and eventually the shadows of my two siblings were no more. Those were the years of the dark stormy clouds gathering and the shadow was obscured and was not to be seen."

"Jim … Jim!"

"Then a young woman appeared from behind a dark cloud, with a smiling face, red cheeks, a black coat with a loose button and rubber boots. As we walked, our shadows were walking side by side and slowly they moved closer and closer until the two shadows merged to one. Our shadow started to sprout and this was the happier time and then there were four shadows. And once again there were the giggles and laughter. The two shadow sprouts grew up and met other shadows and they moved away; but our shadows were dancing with us again.

It was a happy time. The sun was shining twenty-four hours a day and it never rained. The flowers always were in bloom. One day I woke up and there was only my shadow."

"Jim … Jim … what has happened" Madelyn asked?

"How appropriate it is for The Symphony to play Tchaikovsky's 1812 Overture on the Fourth of July."

"What has happened," Madelyn asked?

"I will tell you a little later. I am tired and I will take a short nap."

I must have slept for quite awhile, and when I opened my eyes there was nobody around. "Madelyn, where are you?" "Where did this woman go," I wondered?

I was looking for my cane and it was nowhere to be found. "Darn this woman, she must have taken my cane. I must stand up," I said out loud. I pressed my hand onto the corner of the bench and I stood up without any pain.

I reached for my glasses. "Darn it, she took my glasses too!"

I looked around and everything was clear. The sun was shining, the sky was blue and the birds were happily chirping away, singing their love songs to attract their future mates.

In the distance I saw the outline of a woman walking toward me. As she came closer I saw her smile and her red cheeks; I started to run to close the gap. Yes, she was smiling and was wearing the black coat with her black loose button and black rubber boots.

She cradled my left hand in both of hers, and I touched those red cheeks with the other; they were nice and warm.

My lips touched her lips, and once again our shadows merged together as one.

# The Extras – 3: The Holocaust Images as described by Diana K. Lubarsky

**Second Generation** - The Cover

This is a most difficult sculpture to understand, for in some ways it tries to equate the Shema (a Holy prayer) and the swastika. The older figures in both the front and the back of the sculpture are Holocaust survivors; they are "first generation". The children in the center of this sculpture are second (or third) generation. The children will never quite be able to understand the pain of first generation, and yet they carry the swastika with them. They may smile, and bring along their teddy bears and baseball caps. They may not even yet understand the full implication of what they do. But one of the legacies of Holocaust is that Jews, for all generations, will react to the symbol of the Swastika as the forebearer of unrelenting evil. And as such, the swastika alongside the Shema, has now become a part of the legacy we must pass on to our children. In a most unlikely union both lessons must be learned to insure survival of the Jewish people. And so they all travel forward together, forever on a road paved with faces of the past.

**The Ghetto – Chapter Six**

Birds have landed just outside of the wire that surrounds in the people of the ghetto. The children do what children do. They run to see the birds, and to play. The mothers, however, already sense what is to come next. They huddle together and cry. It is a very sad day for them.

**The Eyes – Chapter Seven**

It is a very old Synagogue, somewhere in Eastern Europe. It is patched and worn and boarded up. There are holes in the old tin roof. But wait, do I see "eyes" staring out between the slats on the back wall? Yes! Who still remains, and why are they there? Were they placed there just before the Synagogue was set afire? Or are they in hiding? Look carefully and you may still catch a glimpse of the Ark, the memorial wall and the serpent-rod symbolic of Moses before it is all lost forever.

**Kaddish – Chapter Eight**

From behind one can see the outlined shadow of the swastika. Certainly that is what led this man to the top of the hill. With certainty it was a Nazi soldier who forced him to dig his own grave. But having reached that point the old Jewish man was granted one moment to make his peace with God. Donning his prayer garments, standing in the sunlight, he recites the mourner's prayers (Kaddish). One can only imagine the wind that began to blow, rippling through his prayer shawl (Tallis) until it flies behind him like the wings of a bird. And at the moment of his death, just as certainly as his body sinks into the grave, his soul takes flight and ascends to Heaven and God.

**Pyramid – Chapter Ten**

There were places in concentration camps where bodies were found in pyramid form as the people climbed upon each other in an effort to escape.

This sculpture symbolizes the holding and touching of humanity doomed. It is inscribed with the Hebrew words meaning, "Hear O Israel!" which is both an angry cry for help and a reaffirmation of faith, even during the last minutes.

**Shoes – Chapter Eleven**

She stands alone and barefoot. She has survived. All that is left from her former life is a single pair of baby shoes. She clutches her stomach and offers the world a silent glimpse of her loss. The three textures of the road converge by her feet to form the letter Shin. It stands for "Shaddai", one of the names of God. It is the artist's way of placing her fate in God's hands. Yet as difficult as her path has been, one cannot help but notice that the pathway before her is broken, foretelling of even more difficulties that lay ahead.

**Mirror – Chapter Thirteen**

He stands on the ruins of his life, which have shattered like the shards of a broken mirror. Reflected in the broken pieces one can see faces and carpeting, books and pieces of furniture. It is all gone, except in the memory of the man. Destroyed. Yet the man still stands. He has survived, and hopefully he will have the strength to re-build.

## Reflections - Epilogue

She is old now. Can you hear the tapping of her foot? There is sadness in her eyes. Fifty-five years ago she was a prisoner in a concentration camp. What is she thinking of today?